ITALIAN CAROUSEL

Andrei Navrozov

Italian Carousel

Scenes of Internal | Exile

HURTWOOD PRESS

First published in Great Britain in 2002
by Hurtwood Press Limited
www.hurtwoodpress.com

A catalogue record for this book is available from the British Library

ISBN 0 903696 43 6

Photographs by Gusov

Sophie de Stempel at work on *Gamblers: Navrozov and Gusov* (2001)

My little helper at the magic lantern,
insert that slide and let the colored beam
project my name or any suchlike phantom
in Slavic characters upon the screen.
The other way, the other way. I thank you.

Vladimir Nabokov, *An Evening of Russian Poetry*

I Rome

Nothing Better to Do

I have always wanted to spend some time in Rome, for a whole rosary of personal reasons. As with much else in a person's private life, to recount these in print is to expose oneself to public ridicule. Yes, Rome is a wonderful city. Yes, the food is good.

But then in England, where I live, the new Labour government came in to finish what the Tories started. And since another famous fact about Rome is that it has already fallen, I figured that over here my chances of being buried under the Eurorubble were encouragingly smaller. So I moved. Days are now passing like centuries outside my window, to the ringing of church bells and the flashing of Japanese cameras.

The paramount joy in all this is a newfound superficiality. On my terrace, in the suggestively Decembrist sunshine, I have been reading a collection of Russian memoirs from the 1830s. How people knew and valued their cities in those days, Petersburg, Moscow, how well they described every façade, every little bridge they had known since childhood! And of course we have all read such memoirs of London, of Paris, of Vienna, even of New York or San Francisco, written by the natural or adoptive children of those cities with the same tenderness, the same observant devotion.

This, alas, is no longer possible. To know a great city like London or Rome nowadays, to know it by heart and in depth and over the span of a lifetime, is to sustain an emotional injury that would render a sensible man all but mute with indignation and shame. Only a giddy foreigner, a pliant, impressionable, superficial stranger, is ignorant enough not to taste the anti-oxidizing agent in his bottle of bubbly *prosecco*; nor has he met enough cranky old-timers to acquire their inevitable bitterness. He knows nothing of the way things used to be fifty, twenty, even ten years back. To him, everything is the real thing.

"The knowledge that the world is ending," wrote a Russian writer in the 1920s, "is what distinguishes an individual from a philistine." In retrospect I am beginning to think that this leave of absence from London, a place over the last thirteen years I had learned to use and to love like the great library it is, was really a convoluted means of getting a few months' respite from living the life of an individual.

Of all the countries I have ever visited, Italy is the only place where one can live like a philistine without wearing trainers, reading the *International Herald Tribune* or degenerating into an animal in other ways. One look in the dining room of a middle-of-the-road hotel anywhere in Europe will remind us that at the moment of pouring anaemic, bluish milk over their bowls of high-fibre cereal, middle-class Swedish, French or Belgian families look exactly alike; that is to say, they look American. They are ready for life in the United States of Europe, where everything will be "better and more fun," as their predecessors in interest used to sing, not always tunefully, aboard eastbound cattle trains.

By contrast, in Italy, philistine life is possessed of an aesthetic so richly ritualized that a Roman pharmacy owner on a week's skiing holiday with his family in Cortina d'Ampezzo will be mistaken for a serious nobleman among serious noblemen. Neither he nor his wife will go skiing, of course; hauteur, like couture, will not be ruffled by rude Teutonic winds; instead, they will join the carefully timed round of cocktails and promenades that exhibit their exquisite, almost hypochondriacal idleness, his languid wit, and her new furs to fine advantage.

Admittedly, the weight of tradition is responsible. The Italian bourgeois had begun to promenade when the aristocracy still fenced and boxed. Now that the middle classes of the world have united, under the colours of Benetton, in Americanism – in sport, most conspicuously, and all the attendant trappings of the sporting life – the Italian is the odd man out. His vision of the active life may be centred on the English country house of a century ago, but unlike Ralph Lauren he never ran and sweated to get there in one generation. To the contrary, the Italian simply promenaded until every *bourgeois* around him turned *gentilhomme*, and now he promenades among them like a great aristocratic original. None of which, incidentally, has deterred Benetton from selling the Brooklyn Bridge to the denizens of Brooklyn, or at least of Brooklyn Heights.

Apart from tradition, which has saved the Italians from the embarrassment of ending up like everyone else, another powerful characteristic that humanizes their middle class is a kind of seriousness, a seriousness which at times resembles cheerfulness and at times cheerful resignation. I have already alluded to the image of life which the Americanist set holds up as a banner of progress all over the world, and I allude to it again in this connection. The familiar strangeness of seeing, on the No. 22 bus in central London, a young woman wearing a track suit or a Walkman is explained by the conjecture that she does not enjoy being on the No. 22, indeed that riding it is only a transitory phase of her existence, and that she would gladly swap this for a run in the park or an evening at the local discotheque. Looking around, one may note that just about everyone else on the bus, including the driver and the conductor, shares her anxiety and her sense of displacement.

What is it with people? From the exodus of the Jews from Egypt to a Sotheby's drinks party, everybody wants to be somewhere, if not something, else. You are talking to an old stupid woman with a glass of champagne in her trembling hand, you think you are being as polite as a boy scout, you suppose the woman is grateful for the attention, but no! You catch her eyeing the door through which a famous used-car salesman is entering, and before you can murmur something suitable ("Madam, is it not time, now that you are in the frosty autumn of your life, to be thinking of higher things?") she is off like a shot. And for the stupid old woman of the parable, read *everyman*, read baker and banker, read newspaper editor and lover, read bootblack and writer.

A scene of this kind, which is routine in New York, Paris, or Peoria, is almost unobservable in Rome and hilariously inconceivable in an Italian provincial town. Of course I would not say under oath that there are no waitresses here who are actually critically acclaimed actresses, and no taxi drivers who have had series pilots produced. But what one observes emanating from each individual soul is extreme, almost sacramental seriousness with respect to its predicament at this or that given moment in time. Until it became the mark of the bourgeois, this solemn self-satisfaction

... as if they had nothing better to do

used to belong to no particular social group and marked equally the upper and the lower classes throughout Europe. A German grain merchant (see Thomas Mann), a Russian nobleman (see Tolstoy), and an English orphan (see Dickens) all saw their position in the world as reasonably convincing, reasonably convenient, and reasonably permanent. The main exceptions were poets, men with bad gambling debts, and Hans Christian Andersen's little mermaid – all tragic and romantic and worthy, yes, but not 99.9% of the population, either.

What I am trying to say is that the seriousness of the Italian way of life, its solemn ritualism and its cheerful acceptance, now accounts for the incredible fact that only in Italy will one see a mother nursing her child or a beggar begging alms or a butcher slicing meat "as if they had nothing better to do." They don't, and in the world as it is today, this is a miracle well worth watching.

II Rome

Where All Belong

I have been trying to describe the noble seriousness of Italian life, remarkable for having given the modern world a middle class with a human face. Even on a simple physical level such as that of the naked eye or of the camera lens, one can observe this seriousness like a uniform glaze all over Rome; so uniform, in fact, that looking at a certain tangible space, say a corner of a market square or a street intersection, one cannot easily distinguish between the very old, the old, and the newer patinations.

A Russian photographer friend who lives in London came to visit for a few days. Generally I hate photography and photographers, and it is quite likely that I love Gusov all the more for being an exception to the rule: so one may delight in having a pimp, a fence, an editor of the *New York Times*, or a circus wrestler among the names in one's address book, and congratulate oneself for being a well-rounded, socially complete person. But Gusov isn't like that, really. Famous in England for his portraits of actors, artists, and musicians, since the death of Princess Diana he has insisted on calling himself a paparazzo.

He also collects combat and hunting knives. During the first day of his stay he trudged dutifully along to all the right places, such as the Colosseum, where the meaning of the phrase "butchered to make a Roman holiday" is usually expected to be revealed, but I could see he was coming unstuck. On the second day he announced he had a terrible stomach ache, angrily waved away a beautifully presented plate of *trippa alla romana* at luncheon, and come evening was frying potatoes in sunflower oil ("No dill," he moaned, "they don't even have dill here!") and drinking warm vodka in the kitchen. I desperately needed to awaken him to the splendour that was Rome, and on the third day we took him to the Pantheon.

Opposite, almost directly beneath the inscription that reads like eternity's e-mail address, M.AGRIPPA.L.F.COS.TERTIVM FECIT, there nestles a small shop with all sorts of junk in the window. A moment later Gusov was singing an animated duet with the proprietor in assassin Esperanto wherein the relative merits of the Spyderco and the Applegate where expounded and compared. He emerged cured, and I saw that what saved him was the proprietor's manifest seriousness, his honest and openly held belief that his knife shop – not the rotunda opposite, not the Egyptian granite of the columns, not the giallo antico and pavonazzeto, not the tomb of Raphael – was the main attraction in the Piazza del Pantheon. And, having emerged thus cured, my savage friend was finally able to traverse the majestic pronaos and even nose around inside Hadrian's marvel without feeling alienated. He now felt he belonged.

Mark Twain, who swore that he would never repeat the phrase about the Roman holiday in his travel notes, lived in an age when the essence of banality was didacticism. In our own age it is incongruity, and one trope the twentieth-century writer might swear to avoid is the city of contrasts.

Contrasts, you see? Contrasts are wonderful, from the modern platitude-monger's point of view, because at the end of the day there is, as it were, no moral.

It is hardly a coincidence that the twentieth century has raised photography to the level of art, so that the very word "contrast" now seems to belong to the darkroom. Photographers thrive on what they flatter themselves believing is Chekhovian ethical neutrality, and what they aim at is popularizing the incongruous at street level. Here is a small man with a big nose, they all like to say, standing next to a big woman practically without one, and behind them is a shiny Cadillac. "So what?" demands an audience of old fuddy-duddies. "So what?! Oh, philistines!" spit back the young artists. "Don't you understand *anything*? This is life in the raw, this is chance, this is nature bursting out of a bookish straitjacket! There are no plots anymore, don't you know, there is only situational chiaroscuro! Look, it's a city of contrasts!"

But as I said, Gusov isn't like that, perhaps because the Russians of my generation still have a sense of intellectual shame. We feel we must wash our hands after picking up somebody else's point of view, even if this means going without dinner. Which is why, having adapted to the city as man and thug, at this moment in his Roman sojourn he came to face a new and even more terrible dilemma, how to adapt to it as man and artist.

We are back to the noble seriousness of Italian life. Rome is not a city of contrasts. Perhaps no city is, but if one's objective is some sort of living truth, not seeing contrasts here is far more vital than not seeing them in New York or Calcutta. Gusov is artist enough to have understood that; and for the second time in those three days I watched him coming unstuck, this time as a photographer. I would like to be able to report that when he first pointed his Nikon at a street corner, Baroque and mildewed and crumbling and covered with Communist graffiti, to photograph a young woman, immaculately elegant, gliding past, his viewfinder melted like pagan bronze in the hands of Bernini; but this did not happen. He looked, and then he looked all around, and then he put the lens cap back on. Like him, the woman belonged.

It was a sentimental, Stalinist moment, rather like something out of a movie about the Civil War when a White officer refuses to shoot a Bolshevik commissar because he too is Russian, or because he too has a soul, or because he too is part of the empire which will someday rule the world for the good of mankind. Those better acquainted with Hollywood depictions of the American Civil War, the civil rights movement or, for all I know, the Holocaust, sexual harassment or intergalactic strife, may substitute this with their own national cinematic clichés, in glorious colour or racially insensitive black and white. The point is, Gusov did not kill the mocking-bird.

The following day being Sunday, we went for a stroll along the Corso. The Romans, in couples or more complex family groups, promenaded, pausing to examine shop windows, and without thinking what this meant we did as the Romans. It meant stopping to look in every shop window on a street of shops that runs from the Vittorio Emanuele monument to the Piazza del Popolo, something like a mile or more. It meant standing for two or three minutes in front of each shop, peering at a display of men's socks that had changed all but imperceptibly since the previous Sunday, discussing, in respectful and leisurely undertone, the nature and meaning of the change. We saw every commercially available sock in Rome, and also all the ties, shirts, shoes, and ladies'

... not to see contrasts here is far more vital

unmentionables. We were very serious, and nobody laughed and said, "Listen, what's wrong with you fellows? Why are you staring at shops you'd never notice in London, even if they were open? And they're all shut, you idiots, on account of it being Sunday!"

Because this was Rome, where we all belonged. The mercer and the cobbler and the dyer had done their best during the week, and the photographer and I and everybody else in town turned out for the performance. Tomorrow it might be the mercer's turn to commission a photographic portrait of his children, my turn to sell an article, and everybody else's turn to do all the other serious things one may do in a community of people who take life seriously and think that every story worth telling must have a moral.

For obvious reasons, politics of the global kind – "democratism," as an English journalist friend of mine has named the modern hybrid of totalitarianism and democracy – is just not one of those serious things. It is for these selfsame reasons that the politically disabled Italians are such a joke among the nations which have lost their sense of humour along with much of their liberty.

III Rome

More Wine, Professor?

There may not be a word for "home" in French, philosophizes Mark Twain in *The Innocents Abroad*, but "considering that they have the article itself in such an attractive aspect, they ought to manage to get along without the word." Who has not seen semantic peculiarities insinuate themselves, with the facility of cognac taken on the terrace, into late-night arguments about race? Of course not all such revelations are always up to the demands of morning logic. Just because the Russians have no word for "toes" does not mean that our foot fingers are more exquisitely shaped than yours, or that we have more of them. Still, it does seem to mean *something*.

The Germans, I am told, do not have a word meaning "efficient." The reason behind this oddity, as all normal lazy people would be relieved to agree, is on the whole pretty clear. The Italians most definitely do not have the word "cheap" (they say "less expensive" or "economical"), and readers of my earlier jottings may reflect that in the mind of a nation that has so attentively preserved the social harmonies of its *borghesia*, from the bass to the alt, nothing in this world comes cheap.

The Russians say, "Fate is a turkey and life's worth a kopeck." Our toes may not be lovelier, but if one wants to use language to pinpoint a national consciousness most hostile to French domesticity, or German efficiency, or Italian prosperity, one need look no further than the Russian word *azart*. It exists in English as "hazard" and in Italian as *azzardo*, but rather than describing the danger of the risk or the risk itself, our word describes the intoxication of the man who risks, the delirious state of mind of a *giocatore d'azzardo*, the gambler's euphoria. As far as I know, no European language can express this nuance, a fact that really ought to lend some credence to the old story about Western materialism and the Russian soul.

Our intellectual attitude to material risk has not changed since Dostoevsky. "However comical it may be that I should expect to get so much out of roulette," he writes, "the routine opinion, accepted by everybody, that it is absurd and silly to expect anything at all from gambling seems to me even funnier." Funny or chilling, but rereading his letters recently, I was able to identify the prototype of the murder victim from *Crime and Punishment* in a German pawnbroker who offered less for his watch than he had hoped to get. He needed the money to play, and his fantasy of killing the old hag right there and then became the spiritual engine of the novel.

Why am I saying all this? Ah, yes. Displacement. My Roman exile, gastronomy aside, is already making me see England as it never was. To put the matter more fancifully, it makes my memory paint situations and scenes, which were undoubtedly episodic, with the kind of improbably broad brush I have seen Italian house-painters use, so that a few minutes into the job all that is left of a room is a Siberia of untraversed, powdery space and some moose hairs stuck to the surface. *Imbiancare* is the word, for those with an interest in comparative handyman semantics. As in London, a half-empty bucket of whitewash is typically left behind, along with some crumpled dust-sheets.

I remember how people would ask me what I was writing, and naively I would tell them the truth. I am writing a book about chance, I would say. "What sort of chance?" they would press on, smelling blood. "Well, as in roulette," I would stammer. Here I think they knew they had me in the palm of their hand, fidgeting like a maimed sparrow. What next, my fine-feathered friend, their dimming eyes seemed to say. Research into prostitution? A study of cocaine? A fresh look at petty thieving? Oh! Navrozov, Navrozov!

The expression "Russian roulette" has lodged itself in the hypocrite's consciousness, and no sooner do I tell an American or an Englishman that I belong to Aspinalls than my dinner-party interlocutor's eyes cloud over with the belief that he knows everything there is to know about me. Yet ninety-nine times out of a hundred, *he*, my interlocutor, is a stockbroker or some other, even more delusional kind of market mooch, just the sort of man Burke had in mind when he wrote, with reference to John Law's financial reformation of France:

> Your legislators, in everything new, are the very first who have founded a commonwealth upon gaming, and infused this spirit into it as its vital breath. The great object in these politics is to metamorphose France from a great kingdom into one great play-table; to turn its inhabitants into a nation of gamesters; to make speculation as extensive as life; to mix it with all its concerns and to divert the whole of the hopes and fears of the people from their usual channels into the impulses, passions, and superstitions of those who live on chances.

By contrast, here in Rome my confession is treated as a professorial whim, and a very distinguished one at that. Ah, *Professore*, you would rather not have the same wine today? You would rather spend the afternoon in the country, finding new stick insects for your private collection? Oh, I understand perfectly, *Professore*. You wish to spend the evening playing a game of chance on the foggy banks of the Thames! May I book you the journey?

Italians respect intellectuals, provided they can afford the wine. Their respect is truly continental, in the sense this is endlessly described in Nabokov's émigré stories of Paris and Berlin, and is essentially the homage paid by an innkeeper to a guest whose eccentric ways are both valuable subjects of local gossip and welcome opportunities for enrichment in the community. The English, to say nothing of the Americans, have all but lost this notion of hospitality where intellectuals are concerned. Tell them you are writing about love and they will think you a child molester. Say it's money and they will decide you are dangerously poor, but if it's poverty that fascinates you, they will despise you as a shady moneybags with republican leanings. Then what *can* a writer legitimately say he is interested in? Small wonder there are so many biographies in the bookstores.

To escape the social consequences and "get respect," one must have rank, accreditation, position. If I could announce, in an Anglophone drawing room, that I am a university professor, in all likelihood my Dangerfieldesque gripe would be no more, no matter how queer my actual or professed inclinations. Well, here in Italy nobody needs to announce that kind of thing. If you can pay for dinner, you are a professor.

... scurrying like mice through the stage set

Which brings me back to my feelings of displacement. Gastronomy and respect for intellectuals aside, I am obviously missing London with its twenty-odd casinos. Rome has none. The other day, walking through a little piazza in the centre of the city, I found myself in a small room packed with at least five hundred people elbowing their way to happiness. "*Che casino, ma guarda che casino!*" one could hear exasperated cries here and there. With the stress on the middle syllable, unfortunately, meaning what bedlam. Bedlam, confusion, *casino* because the most unforgettable thimbleful of coffee in civilization is to be had in this room for about sixty cents – and it's as sure a bet as they come.

Was I happy at the famous Caffè Sant' Eustachio? No. The smoke of Tuscan cigars, the misleading semantics, the pushing crowd had awakened my appetite for the hazards of Mayfair, and I almost burst into sentimental tears from Dostoevskian frustration. "*Portatemi sulle rive brumose del Tamigi,*" I wanted to thunder, whereupon all the imaginary innkeepers of Europe past and present would duly bow and, scurrying like mice through the stage set representing a crooked street, would run to book me an overpriced flight to Heathrow. "*Stanotte voglio giocare d'azzardo!*" I would bellow after them. Nothing but respect for the hero in my Italian melodrama.

IV Rome

Supply and Demand

I have just been to New York, with a stopover in London where we took on board and I was able to read again England's four competing and mutually adversarial "serious" daily newspapers, not counting the specialized *Financial Times*: *The Times*, the *Daily Telegraph*, the *Independent*, and the *Guardian*. None of them is perfect, or perhaps even very serious, on its own, but added together they amount to something without which political life is meaningless and delusional, a culture of broadly polarized debate that is in its own way as miraculous as a great Bordeaux and as much a product of human art as the Trevi fountain.

I am now happily restored to Rome and can hear the famous fountain outside my front door taking in $5000 a week in fives and dimes like one of those maximalist, High Baroque cash registers, all opera-diva curves and flora-shaped curlicues, that they used to have in Woolworth's before the revolution. What revolution, you may ask.

One morning in New York I was having breakfast at the Yale Club in the company of a lively Anglo-Russian child, and looking around the room saw a score of identical broadsheets billowing like the sails of a flotilla of conformity over a sea of watery coffee. "Look, they are all reading the same newspaper!" I exclaimed. There must have been something manic in my voice, because my companion, like a hospital orderly persuading a patient not to throw plates, suddenly grew agreeably philosophical. "It is like everybody in the world cutting wood with the same saw," he said. He wanted to produce an analogy that would highlight the fantastic absurdity of a country where every person who wears a clean shirt and owns cufflinks reads the same issue of an upper-class *Pravda*, while the grubby multitudes just grunt and look at pictures in the *Sun* and the *Sunday Sport*. I suppose he thought the notion of there being just one handsaw for three billion people to share was just absurd enough to keep me calm.

The other social venue of my narrative is Rome's Fiumicino airport, named, significantly, after Leonardo da Vinci, where on my return I drank a small espresso. It was all right. Now, please try to imagine yourself making something for tens of thousands of faceless and nameless foreigners, none of whom you are likely ever to see again and few of whom can taste the difference between good and evil. Would you need to make it well? Would you bother?

And now for the grand synthesis. The revolution I mentioned earlier was really the French Revolution, which could not have occurred without the accompanying assault on the irrational component in the fabric of European life by what is called Reason. It is quite obvious, looking back, that the cultural strands which held human society together had not been spun in the dark satanic mills of the Industrial Revolution, nor bought with paper notes in Adam Smith's free market, nor designed by science for the benefit of all mankind. Concepts like God, duty, honour all come off a different spool, and though this is not historically demonstrable, it is philosophically accurate to claim that the Russian Revolution of 1917 was a logical denouement of the West's effort to bring the backward country in line with the rest of Europe by destroying in Russia what had been destroyed elsewhere since 1789.

This is an inexhaustibly, absorbingly dusty subject, and I only wish to concentrate on a single speck where the two social vignettes with which I began combine into a whole observation. The vulgar adaptations of famous rationalist principles by which the world now lives are legion, as by and by we come to learn that there is no organ in the human body that could conceivably accommodate the soul, that one cannot win at roulette because statistically one must lose, and that virginity is a prejudice that went out with the geocentric model of the universe. The same recent survey in which 19 percent of New Yorkers admitted to having had "group sex" found that what 32 percent of men "looked for in a partner" was an apartment and what 31 percent of women wanted in a man was a car.

But perhaps the most ubiquitous and dastardly of these adaptations is the nursery-school birds-and-bees biologism of supply and demand. Ask a well-meaning, decent, concerned American why there is no other supplier of serious news and opinion in the country besides the *New York Times* and he will tell you that it can only be because there is no call for anything else, mumbling something like "I guess it does the job." This is tantamount to proposing – which, consistent enough with the historical origins of this particular absurdity, is exactly what Darwinists propose – that a camel has two humps because one would be too few and three would be too many. Something exists, *ergo* it must exist; it changes, hence change has been inevitable all along; it becomes extinct, therefore its possible continued existence is not even a matter for discussion.

Here is something I read on the plane on the way over. The author of the article, a well-known British art critic called Waldemar Januszczak, thinks "photography could be the new painting." Why could photography be the new painting? Photography could be the new painting because

> the lively photo-art crowding our galleries has been produced by an impressive array of labour-saving photo-gadgets: digital-enhancement screw-ons, computer solutions, disposable cameras, auto-focus jobs, and all sorts of easily buyable ways of making the production of memorable pictures an effortless process. The result has been a freeing up of photography, and the enfranchisement of all sorts of fascinating artistic imaginations.

All right, you may murmur, he is just another idiot, one of thousands, pay no attention. What is at work here, however, is not so much the pretentious prattling tongue of a random illiterate hack as the invisible hand which seems to direct much of contemporary ratiocination. Leonardo painted because there was demand for Leonardo. Waldemar Januszczak is intelligent because there is demand for intelligent people on newspapers. And of course both are only possible because easily buyable, labour-saving screw-ons have enfranchised their artistic imaginations.

Well, then, why is the espresso at Fiumicino good enough to drink? Silence.

I would define genius as the quality of the human mind which makes a person capable of risk. And risk, by anybody's definition, is neither rational nor prudent. The gnarled little Sicilian

...billowing like the sails of a flotilla of conformity

barista, working the antiquated and gadget-free espresso machine to make coffee when ordinary dishwater would do, has an artistic imagination a million times more powerful than the art critic's. Like Leonardo, he does what he does because he cannot do otherwise, gambling away his time and energy without certain recompense, probably the way his father and grandfather did, and the day he stops will be the day he dies or is replaced by Starbucks. He is, in short, supply incarnate, supply profligate, supply defiant, supply existing independently of demand and testing itself by its own irrational marketing surveys of honour, virtue, and courage.

Everything good in this world, including the world itself, has come from the same source. It is impossible not to become what a Darwinist would call a Creationist upon reflecting that if the universe had not been created by God and was the product of evolution, then all art critics would write like Waldemar Januszczak, all newspapers would be like the *New York Times*, and all coffee would be undrinkable. We are very nearly there, of course, but we have our memories to remind us that things weren't always the way they are and our children to ask us why the airport is named after a Renaissance barman.

V Rome

The Truth About Beauty

Apart from talking about cooking while eating and about eating while not eating, Italians have a favourite subject, a kind of pet peeve, which they touch upon at least a dozen times a day in that same disarmingly artless voice in which the English exchange news of the weather. It is a fact that the English really do talk about the weather, for the simple reason that while the weather in Britain is not as bad as the natives would lead the foreigners to believe – in order to dissuade them from coming to Claridge's wearing Mickey Mouse ears, perhaps, or paying homage to the People's Princess in some other, less honestly felt but equally unsettling ways – it is extremely changeable, and hence a useful subject of conversation. No two Aprils are ever alike, nor two afternoons in any April, nor two hours in any April afternoon, and nobody in London ever saw the same kind of rain twice. It is always smaller, or flatter, or steeper, or softer, or whiter, or longer, or louder than another day's rain, sometimes falling over just half a street, sometimes out of a cloudless sky, sometimes with more than one rainbow over the horizon.

For Italians the perennially newsworthy equivalent is overcrowding. As though guided by the instinct of a swarming bee that leads him to do exactly what everyone else in the city, the province, and the country is doing at that particular moment, an Italian will invariably find himself caught in some obscenely populous swarm, survey it with an air of genuine surprise, and address in its general direction, as if appealing to the errant conscience of each and every citizen worker, the ritual remark: *Troppa gente!* To chide them over this apparent incongruity is like berating bees for their excessive interest in nectar: if you happen to approve of honey, there is nothing excessive about it. Still, it is a little odd seeing a bee point at his fellows with what seems like genuine disapproval and exclaim that he could never imagine so many of them turning out for a sunny afternoon in sweet clover.

One Sunday morning in the spring I found myself inside a small dusty Fiat with four other adults and three children, motionless among similarly freighted cars in the traffic along the Via Aurelia, the ancient Roman road that turns north as it reaches the Tyrrhenian coast and makes its way towards Genoa and on to the Riviera. Tomorrow, a family friend had confided on Saturday evening, is a good day to have lunch in Fregene, but let us leave early because otherwise there will be too many people. It was obvious that by the stroke of midnight on Saturday every friend of every other family in Rome had made the same confidential recommendation. On any other morning the seaside village of Fregene would be twenty minutes away. Like everyone else in Rome, we got there at lunchtime.

Whatever the news of the weather, Englishmen carry umbrellas. Artless as that *Troppa gente!* sounds to the foreigner, it now proved, as I had begun to suspect, so much knowing coquetry. On arrival in Fregene, where the occasional dilapidated villa glimpsed through a wrought-iron gate informs the visitor that the place has seen richer pickings as a fashionable summer resort, I saw an endless avenue of some forty open-air restaurants, each the size of a football field, ready to receive all of Rome on the day all of Rome decides that today is the day for Fregene. The abandoned resort has adapted and become a year-round destination for Sunday outings, attracting enough people for people to start complaining. There was something of Brighton in the old British films about it, but without the penny-pinching sadness, and something of Atlantic City in those same good old days, except I was never there of course and can only guess what that was about.

There was an amazing blonde beauty at the next table in the restaurant we had chosen, a cross between Jayne Mansfield and the dish of spaghetti with *frutti di mare* that had just arrived. I say this in all seriousness, and not only because the shells on my plate reminded me of that famous painting in the Uffizi, but because the sun was burning overhead like magnesium wire and the wine taunted the brain by being judiciously cool, and because there was a breeze from the sea that smelled like wet gravel and dried flowers, and because the dish in question was the work of a great artist and the woman really did resemble the Venus of Botticelli. She was having lunch in the company of two brothers, young men with crewcuts who looked like U.S. Marines, their father, who looked like an ex-Marine, and the other daughter-in-law, who was also auroral in form but only irresolutely 1950s in content, as though infected by some vague worldly sorrow while passing through a Ghirlandaio one morning on her way to the fishmonger's near the Galleria Colonna. There was also the young men's mother, fussing with a baby carriage where a newborn child belonging to one of the women cavorted like the infant Jesus.

Wherever one looked, a similarly tangled and absorbing family scene caught the eye and, once caught, the eye had no choice but to take in the whole Sunday gospel of physical and spiritual wholesomeness, verse after orotund verse. I know I am beginning to sound like a voyeur with strong Nazi predilections, and under ordinary circumstances I might apologize for being charmed by bare arms and golden hair and even Wagner, but in this case I stand my ground. The sheer size of the spectacle before me endowed it with the stature of a natural phenomenon, and most would agree that it is unfair to accuse a geologist (even one obsessed by the health of the Alps) or an astronomer (even one with a romantic fixation on Alpha Centauri) of being a dirty old man and a fascist creep. There must have been eight or nine hundred people around us, which, multiplied by forty, amounted to something like 10,000 happy families crammed into a couple of square miles of blinding sunlight framed by the pale sand and the waveless sea. Gloriously, they seemed all alike, just like Tolstoy said.

Earlier I wrote in these Italian notebooks of mine about a brief trip to New York, and that afternoon in Fregene it occurred to me that during my stay there I had not seen a single beautiful woman. To make the observation more categorical, I would equate beauty with health and simply say that the women I saw in the streets of New York all looked like they were undergoing prolonged chemotherapy. The impression I now have (which admittedly pains the equivocal Russian in me, a Russian brought up on the harmony of Chekhov's ethereal kindness and the counterpoint of Dostoevsky's militant individualism) is that beauty is not merely objective, but collectivist and conformist: more like a doctor's clean bill of health or Italian country cooking or a Mussolini rally

… as though infected by some vague worldly sorrow while passing through a Ghirlandaio

than a clever remark or French *nouvelle cuisine* or a volume of Nietzsche. Why else would all happy families look alike? Why else would anybody come to Fregene?

The lumping of truth with beauty is a characteristically northern, cold-blooded platitude. In reality they could not be further apart, those two, like Moscow and St. Petersburg in the last century: one intimate, cloistered, spontaneous, untidy, the other public, designed, perfumed, splendid. A writer who says to himself "I think this and find it to be true because everyone else does" is a fool and an insult to philosophy, but a lover who thinks "I like her and find her beautiful because others do" is part of the natural order of things and will probably make a good husband. This is because truth lives in cobwebs and musty corners, in interstices and even underground, coming out of a maze of cobbled streets to speak with the tongues of sometime carpenters and country doctors. Beauty is handsomely greying senators and opulently uniformed policemen, it is church bells and brass bands disturbing the nonconformist's sleep, it is spectacularly laid-out thoroughfares, parade grounds and public gardens, in short, it is everything that all the imperial capitals of the world have always done so well. Truth is so original that it resists publication and courts only martyrdom, remaining intensely personal even when of necessity it must become universal. Beauty is an endlessly fascinating exhibition of itself, depersonalized and objective like a set of X-rays marked "Venus," inviting all who would succumb to its open-air, sunlit, and crowded, impossibly crowded vernissage.

A Russian writer I know used to say of Botticelli's allegorical representation of the pagan goddess of love that she looked like a Soviet factory worker, and I would hate to hear what he thought of Jayne Mansfield. I recently watched on Italian TV a clip of Mussolini addressing a beautifully laid-out and splendidly decorated town square, in Turin if I'm not mistaken, on the war in Spain: "Our enemies vow, *No pasaran!* But I tell you, we have passed and are passing!.." And then the camera panned the crowd of thousands upon thousands, and I saw the same scene I witnessed in Fregene, and every woman factory worker was no more sad or sickly than a Hollywood star of the 1950s and every man was as fit and alert as a U.S. Marine. And I am sure that each and every one of them said, as they were getting dressed to arrive in the square no earlier and no later than anyone else in town, that the trouble with these fascist rallies is that there are too many people.

Troppa gente!

VI The Argentario

Local Colour

The promontory of Monte Argentario, billowing on the clothes-line of the Tyrrhenian coast of Italy like a silk shirt held in place by three pins of land, is famous for its summer resort towns of Porto Ercole and Porto Santo Stefano. The shirt, so suddenly lost by so many here in recent political upheavals, is anyhow a suitable symbol of all the historic beachheads of luxury in that furious sea of imprisonments, confiscations, and fines in whose legal depths the betridented taxman has been playing Neptune. As the Italians do everything together, including shopping for silk shirts and talking about going to jail, the Argentario's rivals for the taxman's judicious attentions are not many, and all too easy to rumble. Basically, apart from the moneybags encampment on the Emerald Coast of Sardinia, there is only Positano and the rest of the Capri playground to the south, and Portofino, on the Italian Riviera, to the north. The Argentario is somewhere in between, halfway between Genoa and Naples, and the house I am in is perched on a rocky slope across a small bay from Port'Ercole.

Formally I am in Tuscany, yet the olive and the vine of Chiantishire seem to belong to an altogether different, far less exotic universe. A few minutes inland by car begin the forests and marshes of the Maremma region, "frontier territory throughout history," a local guidebook says. "It was here that the last Etruscan strongholds of the Vulci and Volsini met with the advancing Roman legions. It was Maremma that marked the confines of the Byzantine and Longobard states and it was here that the border between the Papal State and the Grand Duchy of Tuscany was drawn. Today, the same land marks the boundary between Tuscany and Lazio." What this means, in translation from historical euphemism to social topography, is that this is still a refuge for enterprising individualists denounced as brigands, contrabandists, pirates and thieves. Half an hour away, in the mountain fortress of Capalbio, visitors with a romantic craving for roast wild boar are greeted by an effigy of the bandit Tiburzi, who ruled the Maremma until the turn of the century and knew how to eat well. There are conflicting accounts of who betrayed him and why, but lately I think I'm beginning to get the picture.

Our village is ruled by a man called Franco, whose father opened the only bar and restaurant here when grand villas were still being built by the Romans and the Milanese to accommodate the optimism born of Italy's burgeoning black economy. He is a handsome man, with eyes just blue enough to pick up the colours of the sea from the restaurant's terrace, who may be observed sliding a pizza into the oven one minute and talking into one of the three mobile telephones on his corner table the next. Just when he arrives for work is a bit of a mystery, because obviously I'm still asleep, but he never leaves the restaurant before two in the morning, when we drink our last Averna together. Here I must announce that in the course of the last two years, since I first met him, I have come to the inescapable conclusion that he is the only man in Italy endowed with what a

Russian, an Englishman, and an American could all agree is a sense of humour. Hence he is the only Italian I always take seriously, even when he isn't joking.

Mine is not, I hasten to add, a hysterical case of hero worship, a kind of Patricia Hearst fascination with her own captors or a Soviet housewife's belief that Molotov is sexually irresistible. Yet the truth is that all the summer rentals in the village are handled by Franco on commission, and the query most often overheard at the beach, second only to *"Cosa mangiate?"* or *"Dove andate stasera?"* (we get very few foreigners here), is the vital question of why the wife of this pharmaceutical company president from Bologna or the mistress of that chewing-gum magnate from Turin had been reckless enough to make her own arrangements, instead of "renting through Franco," only to be reduced to a quivering bundle of nerves even before the season started. This evidence of power, naked enough to make captains of industry blanch and their spouses tremble, has two notable consequences.

One of these is best observed in the Mediterranean sun of the early afternoon. It is difficult to get local colour right, of course. That burning white hole in the cool blue enamel, inappropriately, always reminds me of a Russian poet who wrote that he was lonely

as the last good eye
of the man who has gone to live among the blind.

Anyway, come early afternoon, Franco sits under the canopied entrance of the bar surrounded by past, present, and future clients, dispensing advice and succour in the manner of some medicine man or scribe in the shade of a baobab tree, or a mango grove, or… Well, you know what I mean. Think the East, think the nexus of India and Africa, think Somerset Maugham, think Asprey of London. Yes, it is notoriously difficult to get local colour right. I note, for instance, in a copy of the *New York Times Magazine* that has floated by me on the beach like a letter in a bottle, that the recipe for Balinese Tuna Salad calls for one and a half teaspoons of kosher salt. Now, *that* can't be right. What I am trying to say, I suppose, is that all the prattle of the baobab and the mango is here to suggest that there are some fundamental ways in which Italy is closer to Borneo than to Manhattan.

A pomegranate grove, perhaps? Such trees do grow here, so *that* is right, but the real point is that those who did not "rent through Franco" shall never enter the pomegranate grove. At least until dinner time, while the sun is still high overhead and they are still in their sporty shorts and natty slippers, Italian men are hypochondriac, melancholic, and easy prey for some of the pettiest household paranoias. If their sewer is backing up, they immediately blame their wives for not having "rented through Franco." Their wives are not far behind when it comes to being suggestible, and if the cistern suddenly has no water one can be sure that the husband will be excoriated, by both the wife and the mother-in-law on the premises, for his characteristic obstinacy in supposing that he knew best when he dealt with the owner directly instead of "renting through Franco." And so it happens that those who believed they did good, those arrogant men of worldly influence in distant Milan or Bologna, those bejewelled women with perfect blonde highlights in perfect blonde

… mine is not a hysterical case of hero worship

hair, are now outcasts, pariahs without protection from the vagaries of nature and fate, social flotsam without access to Franco, condemned to the outer reaches of the bar while the meek inherit and have their refrigerators promptly fixed.

The revolutionary, retributive or at least redistributive overtones of Franco's enterprise, based though it is entirely on the power of suggestion, account for the second of the observable consequences I mentioned. Everyone, rich or poor, has something to say about him behind his back. Typically, the rich say he belongs to the mafia, and when I object, pointing out that he neither drills holes in people's cisterns nor sneaks into houses to tamper with their ancient Italian refrigerators, they put on a thin, sad smile and look away.

The poor are less predictable, perhaps because envy is a finer emotion than fear. Recently the master of a nearby riding school, who had been told I was a friend of Franco's, came up and addressed me as follows: "*Buona sera, Signore.* You are a friend of Franco's. Well, let me tell you something. I've got more brains in this little finger on my left hand than Franco has in his entire body."

Excuse me? I said, trying to inject as much of the Valley Girl as I could into what was genuine astonishment, *e allora*? "Well, I've known Franco thirty years, and I just wanted you to know that he is not as clever as he thinks he is. He didn't get where he is by his intelligence." But don't you see that he works like a dog, that he's worked like a dog for all those thirty years, and that this may have had something to do with his success? "Sure he works. But he's got the whole village in hand!" Well, he is an aspiring monopolist, which is another name for a good businessman. Without him, there would be nothing here, true? "True," he conceded grimly, affecting the liplessness of the rich. Because everybody would fight, everybody would quarrel with everybody else, and then the big boys would arrive and build a giant resort hotel for a lot of fat Germans, which would probably close down in a few years. You would have your social justice then, but who would take riding lessons?

I saw that he was unconvinced. In his heart the riding instructor hoped that the whole Argentario would one day be drowned in burning sulphur, if only to prove that the aspiring monopolist was not as clever as everyone thought.

VII The Argentario

Italian Lessons

Two or three times a week, after dinner, I watch the traffic jam outside Franco's bar. What causes it nobody knows, but a perfectly ordinary intersection of two perfectly ordinary country roads is suddenly blocked. Nobody knows why the best watermelon is the one with the smallest spot on the bottom, or how come the tastiest tomatoes are always misshapen, or what it is about myrtle leaves that causes a suckling pig to be so marvellously tender. It's just one of those things, and anything other than simply accepting it is every bit as foolhardy as wondering why the Northern Line is the one to avoid when travelling on the Underground in London, or why American college professors like cheating on their wives.

Although at most three vehicles, and seldom more than a dozen persons, are involved in the ensuing commotion, in the dilating twilight it is never clear who is behind the wheel of which car. The actors and the spectators are quickly amalgamated, as the passengers and the drivers get out and take up the parts of victims, witnesses, experts, and jurors. Though less contrived than the Report of the Warren Commission or a James Fenimore Cooper novel, their mutually inconvenient entanglement is as picturesque as any to be found this side of pure fiction. Since I do not drive, and the impartial truths of motoring are hidden from me – much as the truth of music is hidden from many people who assume that he plays best who plays loudest – I usually think the driver of the car that has the prettiest girl in it is the villain, who ought to be thrown in jail as a matter of public safety. But my own opinion in the matter is beside the point. What I come to the bar to savour is the escalation of hostilities on all sides, which, Italy being Italy, always follows a pattern.

The very first of the many names which one Christian is likely to call another in such situations here would fall, in English, Russian, or any other language or culture of which I have even the scantiest knowledge, under the narrow rubric of grave insult, usually anatomical or scatological in form. There follows what appears to be a ruminative pause, during which the participants evaluate and focus their invective before proceeding to the next level of calumny, still more unprintable and, to any but the Italian ear, still more barbarous. This almost mandatory intermission, like the traditional interval in the theatre, allows the machinery of stagecraft to project a new mood, as shirt sleeves are rolled down, trousers pulled up, cigarettes stubbed out, and rear-view mirrors are demonstratively tweaked. Now references to sexual practices, gender uncertainties, and genealogical defects of every kind are flung right and left, obscene fulminations rending asunder the gentle, echoless dusk of Tuscan summer until the next mandatory interval once again shrouds the scene in silence.

And there ends the second act. Mind you, we are not at the point when the plush seats empty, and refreshments, champagne and smoked salmon on toast, are taken by the weary in the buffet. We are not at the point when the less plush use lavatories, fan themselves with playbills, or pore over the list of corporate sponsors to kill time. We are, rather, at the point at which any man or woman outside of Italy, no matter how mildly mannered, is already mad as hell, and would be quite prepared for as much physical violence as might be justified in the eyes of his or her culture. A bleeding nose, a cheek lacerated by a manicured fingernail would be the kind of bargain price one would expect to pay, under less velvety skies and on a night not as deep as this indigo, for verbal provocations so extreme.

Instead the curtain rises to reveal a stage emptied of all movement, where only the crickets, in the orchestra pit below the bar's terrace, keep on grinding out their Buddhist hymn to forbearance. A passing mongrel dog, infected by the excitement of an otherwise supperless evening, barks in the audience like an old man clearing his throat on an old recording. And then it comes. It would be tempting, but I think misleading, to say that it sounds operatic, like something out of *La Forza del Destino* or that blood-curdling shriek in *Rigoletto* when the jester discovers that his daughter is the body in the sack. No, it is simply spoken, never shouted, and it always comes perfectly enunciated, like a great line from Racine:

"*Maleducato!*"

The word is the awful forbidden, and the uttering of it is the whole third act and final denouement of the performance I would happily attend every night of the week, if Franco could organize it and charge admission. What can it possibly mean, this most awesome of taboos, this sacred malediction spat in the face of a suspected perpetrator of traffic congestion? What is it, this most potent of curses, used long after all other means of abuse have been exhausted and it is clear to all, including the stray dog, that the malfeasant in question is both an impotent born of a promiscuous mother and a racial aberration sired by a whole gallery of sexual deviants? What is this lethal bite of the Italian imagination's hydrophobic echidna? The Collins Sansoni Dictionary says "I. *a.* rude, impolite, ill-mannered, ill-bred. II. *s. m.* (*f.* -a) rude person."

If one could rely on dictionaries, of course there would be no reason to sit in the bar and watch a lot of people who are as mad as hell or, in other words, in an emotionally and hence culturally revealing predicament. What I find so remarkable, and the Collins Sansoni cannot convey, is the extent to which the Italians have learned to make a spectacle, as well as a virtue, of being cartoon-character predictable. This is a trait which their common spoken language, artificially disseminated at the expense of the local dialects since the unification of Italy, but most ruthlessly since the advent of national television, at once belies and encourages, with bizarre consequences.

It is wrong to claim that in order to understand the English as they are today, one must master the literature their ancestors created centuries ago; far more instructive, perhaps, to absorb their journalism of the last forty years. To understand the modern Russians, one need not learn their verse; their Soviet political heritage is far more relevant. But the plain fact is, whatever the cultural antecedents, that an analogous brawl in Birmingham or Chelyabinsk would not run along plot lines that were known long in advance, rehearsed many times over, and familiar to all the native participants since childhood. Similarly, if you happened upon an English or a Russian girl standing in front of a shop window, looking at blouses or shoes the way women do, you would not

...as much physical violence as might be justified in the eyes of his or her culture

be able to guess her innermost thoughts if your life depended on it. Only a Shakespeare or a Chekhov could put them in words, now as centuries ago, with any plausibility or veracity:

MEDVEDENKO: Why do you always wear black?

MASHA: Because I am in mourning for my life. I am unhappy.

"*Che belle scarpe!*" is the Roy Lichtenstein thought bubble above the young Italian's gracefully inclined head. She is not permitted to have any other text in the caption by dint of her culture, her upbringing, and her manners, any more than she is permitted to call a driver impolite within the first three-quarters of an hour's argument in the street. Of course I cannot swear that the text is one hundred percent invariable, since she may well be thinking, "*Che carine!*" or "*Che meraviglia!*" when she looks at the shoes, much as in the dramatic denouement at Franco's bar one may sometimes hear a variant "*Disgraziato!*" or "*Ignorante!*" But a thought bubble is what it is, not much room for thought there to begin with, and hardly a suitable place for anything really unexpected.

The Shakespeare and Chekhov of the synthetic language spoken by modern educated Italians throughout Italy is not Dante or Pirandello but Dottoressa Paola Rosa-Clot, Professor of Foreign Languages at the University of Turin, author of the Linguaphone *Corso d'italiano*. Here is something from a lesson entitled "The Fashionable Friend," which I take to be the rough equivalent of the opening lines from Chekhov's *Seagull* quoted above. Two women are discussing a pair of shoes one of them bought in a sale, and the irony is that the other thinks the heels might be a little too high:

RAFFAELLA: Che belle scarpe! Dove le hai comprate?

LUCIANA: Le ho prese in una svendita… Ti piacciono?

RAFFAELLA: Sì, ma come fai a camminare con dei tacchi così alti?

LUCIANA: È un po' difficile, ma sai, sono di moda.

I cannot restrain myself from dipping into "Sightseeing in Rome," where a woman asks her companion whether the Colosseum was built with the sole aim of putting Christians to death:

GRAZIELLA: Era usato solo per far morire i Cristiani?

GIOVANNA: No, per ogni sorta di spettacoli sanguinosi.

Do people really talk like this? Here they do. I think I have heard this very exchange on more than one occasion among Italian tourists now thronging to Rome, as if it were a finishing school for Italianness, to round off their conversational skills before all the *maleducati* arrive from abroad, all those funny, unpredictable strangers with highly unfashionable knapsacks and improperly modulated curses.

And if I haven't, I'm sure to hear something very much like it before the stroke of Millennium.

VIII The Argentario

The Princesses and the Pea

The sun is no longer the hot buttered pancake worshipped by the ancient Slavs, it has been reformed into an altogether more Christian, lenten, and distant figure. The sea is still beautiful, though it too no longer moves with the same pagan frankness, its orgiastic, by turns manic and depressive, barometrically motivated summer feasts and famines having given way to that reflective coherence of cloistered life which a weekend visitor, who has not personally witnessed the seasonal conversion, is likely to misconstrue as stormy gloom. Wherever you look, royal aquamarines and emeralds in the Argentario's crown are being switched for Siberian opals and beryls, and despite the cheering news that the substitution cuts down the cost of being embosomed in some of the most expensive nature on the Tyrrhenian coast, all the terraces are now emptying, Filipino maids are handing in the keys, and even I am making inquiries about where to go next.

Franco is working on it with all the aplomb of "*Ci penso io!*" for which the Italian service sector is justly famous. This is a combination of "I'll see to it, just leave it to me, I have your interests in mind, everything will be taken care of, we understand each other, I know just what you're looking for, don't you worry about anything, I've got a friend, he has a cousin, they have an uncle" with the underlying sense of "And if in the end I should fail, we'll have a good laugh about it, won't we?" The hero of my last two entries from the Argentario, Franco likes to play the quintessential southern nepotist while achieving his ends by hard work, which he does in secret, and by endless telephoning. Some years back I read an article about a Robin Hood of a confidence man who ran an elaborate pyramid scheme for the benefit of the very people he was swindling all over America, so that a free car would be procured for one client at the expense of another, both clients having had to pay the price of a third client's free pleasure cruise. This side of madness and the law, Franco is the nearest equivalent of that American: he has just sent faxes detailing my predicament to every real-estate agent in Siena while telling me that he is well-acquainted with the city because he used to visit a girl there with splendid, let us say, results.

Last year I made the mistake of telling the social grandees of Porto Ercole, who wanted to know whither their charming Russian acquaintance once the sirocco starts, that I wanted to spend some time in Rome or Florence, and that "Franco is working on it." Franco? Ha-ha-ha, they laughed bitterly, that fellow Franco has a long arm, nobody can deny that, but surely not as long as their own Rome or their cousins' Florence. Tee-hee-hee, tinkled young Count Cucciolini. Hoo-hoo-hoo, boomed Duke Ognibrontolo. Ho-ho-ho, hooted Prince Dotto dei Settenani. Why don't I speak to *their* cousin, or daughter's friend, or daughter's friend's agent? *That* would be wise. Because to rent a summer place, like all those despicable film producers and glorified grocers who are jacking up prices all over the place, a local fixer may be enough, but when it comes to residence in town thank God one must still be presented to society.

I did speak to them, and the scenario was invariably the same. After a while I began telling the grandees "Franco is working on it" just to get their goat, so hilariously indignant and flustered did they become at the thought of his arm lengthening, like the shadow of the spectre that is haunting Europe, to reach into their ancestral domain and pocket a fat commission. Yes, I would insist with feigned bonhomie, Franco will find me a place, I'm sure. No, your friend's cousin's house didn't work out, because first of all she is deaf, though not so deaf as to desist from bargaining, and secondly she said she didn't want to move out because her mother's things were in the house and she couldn't bear the thought of other people touching them. But don't worry, Franco will find something sooner or later. He says he is working on it.

No, that noble lady's brother-in-law's friend's recommendation didn't work out either. The place was too small and had no terrace, though like all the apartments in the inescapable scenario it was tucked into an amazing Roman palazzo overlooking an architectural monument of still greater antiquity. It was a brilliant morning in early October, I stood by the window admiring the view and said I would take it, and no sooner were the words out of my mouth than the owner raised the price we had agreed by telephone just the night before. In her mistaken, though obviously not newly acquired, belief that useless information is a fair alternative to straight dealing, she explained to me that her ailing husband, who had just left for the airport, begged her, simply begged her, not to let anyone, not even the charming Russian acquaintance of her dear friend in Port'Ercole, have the apartment for less.

That evening I'm at the bar as usual for an aperitif and a gossip with Franco. "Ah, *pisellino*," he greets me, enjoying my customary uncertainty about whether a little pea is quite as endearing a thing to be called as the other little thing is offensive, "*come andata?*" The princess tried to pull a fast one, I tell him. "Did you show the old bag you liked it? You stood by the window and admired the view of some broken stones? Still greater antiquity? Nothing is of greater antiquity than *la principessa*, my friend! *Pisellino*, what did I teach you?" He gets up from the table and begins to recite: "*Al contadino*" (here he always raises the index finger of his right hand) "*non far sapere*" (pause) "*come è buono*" (mischievous twinkle) "*il cacio con le pere*" (triumphant laughter). Which, in the didactic style of another century, we may render as follows:

> From Farmer hide, lest he gets Airs,
> How excellent his Cheese with Pears.

Anyway, for this, that or another reason it would by then be perfectly clear that yet another Roman palazzo, or yet another vaulted gallery with frescoed walls and a Jacuzzi, or yet another Fiesole villa with a musical fountain that is also a clock, was but an unattainable social mirage and the whole scenario would repeat itself, I goading the nobility of Port'Ercole with Franco's ever-lengthening arm and they sending me on an ever-wilder goose chase. Meanwhile, time was running out, and Franco seemed to be spending night after night on his many mobile phones without any apparent result.

...the apartment where I began writing this diary last year

Then one day in November, with the sirocco long in place, terrace umbrellas all folded, and even the bar officially closed except to make me a morning cappuccino, at last Franco ordered me into his Asti Spumante or whatever his spiffy car is called. We were bound for Rome, for the apartment – two terraces on two floors overlooking the Trevi fountain on one side and, no less crushingly undeserved, the Baroque façade of the church of San Vincenzo on the other – where I began writing this diary last year. The owner was a very tanned middle-aged man, his hairy arms covered with interesting tattoos, who lived there with his wife, his two teenage sons, and his mother-in-law. While the elderly lady and her daughter, relegated to the kitchen background, were rolling the pasta and cutting the smoked pig's cheek for an *amatriciana* that I will remember for as long as I live, the owner, the agent, and the little pea of a woebegone tenant were working out the finances with a broken ballpoint pen on a paper napkin. This done, both parties licked their thumbs and, laughing at the grimy imprints, affixed them to the grand total with mock solemnity.

A contract? Aw, have another helping, my friend. A security deposit? Pfph, what for, I know where you live! How to pay? In *sterline*, of course, from beautiful foggy London with those marvellous bridges! When can I move in? As soon as we've moved out! And, as readers of this journal already know, that's exactly how it all turned out. And need I add what a fabulous boon it was, being able to ask all those Port'Ercole grandees to drinks on the terrace, waiting… waiting… waiting to be asked the six-billion-lire question… and by the way how did you find this amazing place… oh well do you remember Franco… yes well but I told you he would find me something suitable in Rome… yes he found it straight away… yes a single telephone call. Curtain. A shocked audience. A huge line at the coat-check.

But what every picaresque social comedy needs is a sobering afterpiece. The tattooed owner of the apartment in the Piazza della Fontana di Trevi, as I learned by chance on my last day there, is out on bail and awaiting trial for his part in the assassination of an associate of the Vatican banker Calvi, the man found hanged under Blackfriars Bridge in London some years ago. Although on me personally this piece of news had the salutary, and not entirely familiar, effect of rushing to make sure that all outstanding utility bills had been paid, as far as Franco is concerned there is nothing more sinister here than a funny coincidence. And as the sirocco begins to bear down on the exposed village on the Argentario hillside I can hardly wait to hear what this year's frantic telephoning will bring.

IX Florence

Papal Soap

The domiciliary organ of the host to which I have now attached myself is the cavernous Renaissance of every spiritual parasite's dreams, most of it still inhabited, in that *Cherry Orchard* kind of way which keeps grand English country houses tottering but not always falling to the National Trust, by the descendants of the Florentine merchant prince who, in 1620, bought what was then the Palazzo Acciaiuoli, designed by Buontalenti shortly before he completed the Palazzo Uffizi. Some years later the family acquired from the waning Medici the much larger Casino di Parione, which became their principal residence and is today the most important private museum of art in Florence. The lesser palace, however, has a private park, a Baroque jewel set in box and lemon by Gherardo Silvani, where I can stroll, pick persimmons, and occasionally think of something to write in my journal.

Naive as this may seem to anyone who has made a day trip to Florence or owns an encyclopaedia, for the moment I do not want to name the princely family. The fig leaves carefully placed, at some sticky historic juncture, on all the male statuary in the palace once known as the Casino di Parione, which now bears the family's name, do not diminish the pleasure of the proceeding. There is a hint in this for our times, one which I myself heeded but little in the course of a perversely frank and shamelessly prolonged adolescence. Now I know better. Unfortunately I'm joking, but anybody within a hundred miles of Machiavelli's tomb will tell you that it is a good policy to keep your trap shut until you get out of town.

Anyway, since then the family have produced a capable fifth-period pope and acquired a first-division mediaeval saint. The fact that this is Stakhanovite even by local standards is illustrated by the following embittered reminiscence. A few months ago, at a drinks party in London, I ran into an outrageously beautiful girl who had two cardinals and a pope in her family, which I thought, and a Roman friend concurred, was as good as it ever gets. And, merely because of this cruel twist of genealogy, even though Paola Aldobrandini was in town all on her lonely own doing a course in computer science, we felt too timid to ask her to dinner that evening. Thank you, Clement VIII.

Now that I am here in Florence we do not even count the cardinals, who are like the small change of copper-yellow chanterelles in the mossy path of a mushroom picker looking for high-denomination cepes. *What are you going to find next if you keep on like this*, is the prevalent attitude, *aldermen?!* I must say, however, that the socially impartial daughter of the present princess – to whose lares and penates or, more to the point, apartments overlooking the Silvani maze, I am parasitically attached – lets drop with breezy modesty that a pope in the family is always the hard part. Once you've got your pope, she says, he can fix you up with a plausible enough saint, if that's what you really want, or put your escutcheon on top of a grandiose public monument, if this is your line of ambition. She says the reasons for why that should be so are on the whole pretty obvious, and since the dining room in which she says it is dominated by the portrait of her very own S. Andrea, by no less persuasively mythopoeic a hand than Guido Reni's, all I can muster by way of reply is a feeble nod followed by a sycophantic chuckle.

The princess gets pretty steamed up on hearing of her daughter's flippancy, or ignorance as she calls it, since the plain fact is that the family saint, who died in 1374 ministering to victims of the plague, was canonized in 1624 by Urban VIII, many years before the family pope was born. The ancestral proverb she quotes as she vents her displeasure is *boni sì, ma santi più* (which may be translated from the language of the epoch as "be as good as you like, but let's not have any more of this saints stuff"), referring to the well-documented story that Pope Urban made the family foot the bill for historical research into the life and miracles of their beatified ancestor, an idler, drunkard, wencher, and gambler who became a Carmelite monk and later Bishop of Fiesole. Which is already pretty miraculous, if you ask me.

On the other hand, Urban VIII belonged to the Barberini, who, though originally Sienese, enjoyed an equally well-documented association with their Florentine fellow clansmen that eventually resulted in intermarriage. So maybe the young cynic is not so much off the mark, her flippancy buoyed by the realization that in a single century culminating in their pope's prelacy, whammo (which may be translated from the language of the epoch as *mirabile dictu*), no fewer than three boys in the family grew up to be cardinals. It's who you know, basically.

But I seem to have strayed. These jottings of mine, after all, are not so much about the past as about the present. And the daily question I ask myself is why I am taking such personal interest in all this, and why all the back-and-forth between mother and daughter, and all the family crests and relics and lemon trees and paintings and personalities and faces, should be giving me such a thrill. Why should I, a Russian who has spent half his adult life in England, be suddenly feeling like an American tourist who accidentally got his snout into some fabulous trough of Yurrupeen culcha? Is not my England a nation whose aristocracy is still legally a vital agent of the body politic? It is, unlike republican Italy. Is not my friend Harry descended from the Henrys of Shakespearean history? His country estate is every inch as encyclopaedic. And what of my London neighbour, Katarina? No less *sfarzoso* a personage than Queen Victoria is her ancestor on both her mother's and her father's side. Do I preen like an Upper East Side matron, blab nonsense like a Yale student, and chuckle sycophantically like a homosexual decorator when I talk to them, too?

Because on the face of it, as I say, this way of life is no different from what one can easily find in any number of English country houses – of equal, if not greater, antiquity and distinction – and occasionally even in London. The last time I saw Harry he was buying ice-creams for the children from a vendor in the middle of a trailer park. The first time I saw Katarina, she was cleaning our communal drain dressed in a nightgown and rubber boots. Here the prince, I have the distinct impression, has grown a beard because there is not enough hot water to shave with in the mornings. Here the princess is a whirling dervish, fighting wool-eating moths, social-climbing suitors, tax-gouging authorities, and other forms of systemic entropy that threaten the next generation with destitution. Here old retainers shuffle aimlessly through corridors, ostensibly on their way to mend a curtain or to adjust a fire screen. Here doors squeak, roofs leak, and letters from Sotheby's lie unopened.

… a private park, a Baroque jewel set in box and lemon

The young prince runs a country estate that produces an excellent Chianti and olive oil: in England it would be turnips and rape-seed, unless the place made more money as a conference centre. One daughter has married and moved to Rome: this would be London, unless it was New York, Paris, or Rome. The other two daughters, who live here, are painters: just what they would be if they were called Somerset, unless they became sculptors or writers. One is married to a Venetian: she would be married to a Venetian if she were English, of course, unless he happened to be Florentine. In short, what is the difference? Why do I giggle and blab and preen?

The answer comes to me one morning as Lucia, one of the old retainers who has been doing the washing in the family since the merry days of Pius XI, shuffles up to say that we are out of soap. Since the ensuing conversation is revelatory, I record it in its entirety. LUCIA knocks on the outer door of the study. "Yes?" LUCIA knocks once more on the inner door. "Enter!" Enter LUCIA. She stands by the door, arms by her sides, head slightly bowed.

I: Good morning, Lucia. What is it?

LUCIA (approaching): Good morning, sir. I have spoken to the princess, who has directed me to speak to the lady of your house... With whom I already spoke yesterday, but... She is not here today, and... Will you permit me to speak with you of this matter?

I: Yes, of course. *What* is the matter?

LUCIA: As you certainly do not know, sir, because you cannot possibly know, although perhaps you do know because it pleases you to acquire knowledge of such matters, I do your family's laundry. This is done by immersing different things, which we call *clothes* – although, on occasion, these may be bedclothes, such as sheets, or simply towels, such as you would find in the bathrooms here and there, in short, everything made of fabric that is used, and becomes soiled from one day to the next – into a quantity of boiling water with soap.

I: Very well, I understand perfectly. And?

LUCIA (nervously) : I have been doing my job for almost two weeks now... I trust to your satisfaction.

I: Of course, of course. But what *is* the matter?

LUCIA: The soap is finished.

I: All right then, let's buy some! We'll get some more this afternoon. It's the stuff in big square boxes, right? Powder?

LUCIA: Bravo, sir! May I say, sir, well done! How astonishingly well you understand practical issues! And may I add that the lady of your house, divinely beautiful as she is, understands them equally well. And your child is perfectly beautiful also, and of course sharp as a blade... That's what we say in the country when we want to describe someone as very, very clever.

I: Thank you very much. It's because we don't own a television and don't send him to school.

LUCIA (gasps): Ah, sir. How true it is what you say! When I was a young girl, I did the washing for the Counts N— and it was the same, always private tutors for the young ones. How courageous you are, and what a pleasure it is for me to be working for a master who is so good.

I: Thank you, Lucia, I promise you we'll get the soap!

Lucia (retreating): Thank *you*, sir! And please give my sincerest thanks to the lady of your house when she returns!

I invite readers who may have some doubt as to what makes this exchange so damn revelatory to compare it with a diary entry made ten years ago in *The Journals of Woodrow Wyatt*, just published in England to much scandalous recrimination. The late Lord Wyatt, a vizier to both Mrs. Thatcher and the Queen, recounts an anecdote about the 10th Duke of Marlborough, next to whose granddaughter he finds himself seated at dinner. The thing to listen for here is Wyatt's tone of proletarian incredulity, worthy of *Pravda* in my own grandfather's day:

> That was when Bert Marlborough stayed with his daughter in America and came down to breakfast and said: "There is something wrong with my toothbrush. It didn't foam this morning." It was then established that he was travelling without his valet who always put the toothpaste on the brush for him. It seems that he was unaware that this is what caused the foam in his mouth.

I rest my case. I do not think there's anybody in England – including the oldest retainers in the grandest country houses in the remotest counties who came up to London for the Coronation and have not been back there since – that still talks, acts, and thinks like our Tuscan laundress. And for this reason, even if the aristocracy should legally remain a vital agent of the body politic in England, its eminence is and will always be illusory.

Here it is real, which is why spiritual parasites of every description, from American housewives and homosexual decorators to Chiantishire colonists and itinerant idlers, will chuckle and blab and preen for as long as Lucia's generation is alive. She is what makes the princess a princess, and Italy – Italy.

X Florence

Something of Art

In *Something of Myself*, his 1935 autobiography, Kipling remembers that when he was a young man, working for the English newspaper in the Punjab, "I no more dreamed of dressing myself than I did of shutting an inner door or – I was going to say turning a key in a lock. But we had no locks." Then follows a definition of ultimate luxury, "luxury of which I dream still." It is a definition which I have tested on a number of persons of my acquaintance, if only to see whether they would be able to comprehend it in all its vastness, and all of them have admitted that they cannot. With the reader's permission, I shall keep the magician's white handkerchief draped over the bird cage for a few moments longer.

In a recent issue of *Vanity Fair* magazine, a man introduced as "a top information-age entrepreneur" – which is how one might think of introducing Lorenzo de' Medici – describes how he bought himself a private jet. He writes anonymously, because to his top information-age mind the shame of being thought a sybarite is greater than the exultation of being considered rich. Indeed, much of the story of his $12 million purchase and refurbishment of the Gulfstream III (yes, an interior designer called Ms. Guice puts in an ostensibly long-legged appearance) is a kind of college sophomore's simulacrum of a moral argument involving a furtive, shamefaced, mournfully subjective conscience (which asks, "who was I to spend this kind of money on myself?") and a boastful, big-mouthed, practical necessity (which induces him to pay $36,000 "for two flat-screen TVs"). Finally he drops the name of Warren Buffett, one-of-the-world's-wealthiest-men, who has christened his private plane *The Indefensible* "as partial penance for the incongruous luxury." Ah well, iss aw right then, innit, as fashionable people say nowadays in the Royal Borough of Kensington and Chelsea.

Kipling was nothing if not honest, both as a writer and as a man, and there is no reason to doubt that while in Lahore he never worked less than ten and "seldom more than fifteen" hours a day, despite persistent fever and chronic dysentery. "I discovered," he recalls, "that a man can work with a temperature of 104, even though next day he has to ask the office who wrote the article." Typhoid and cholera were rampant, and "death was always our near companion." At the start of his six-year stint on the paper, his salary was 100 rupees a month. He was only able to return to London after managing to flog the copyrights to *Plain Tales from the Hills* and *Departmental Ditties* to a native "who then controlled the Indian railway-bookstalls." In short, I would wager that the colonial journalist had more stamina in his little finger than the top information-age entrepreneur has in his whole wallet. Luxury is not necessarily enfeebling.

Even the ultimate luxury experienced by Kipling, which was... Reader, beware. I am being perfectly straightforward. I am not about to drop some relativistic paradox of the Russian soul school from Tolstoy to Solzhenitsyn, where a drink of water and a crust of bread are like the costliest wines and viands, where a man bereft of everything discovers the joy of the smallest something, where a once proud and powerful *bon vivant* experiences ecstasy in a jail cell as his body begins to absorb the almost human warmth of a rude wooden stool. No, the ultimate luxury experienced by Kipling was that every morning his valet would enter the bedroom while he was asleep bearing the razor and the soap, approach his master's bed with feline, Machiavellian tread and, without so much as a creak of a floorboard, begin to lather his cheeks.

"I was shaved before I was awake!" Can the top information-age entrepreneur fawned over by *Vanity Fair* get his sophomoric conscience around that one? Can I, a sincere sybarite in the closing years of the twentieth century? Can anyone out there? But the real problem, of course, is not one of conscience. The problem is that in the closing years of the twentieth century nobody can find a professional barber even in a barbershop – in London I once had a shave at Trumpers, the sole surviving gentlemen's establishment in Curzon Street, with an aesthetic result as disastrous as the spiritual wounds were enduring – while any prospect of engaging a valet who happens to be an amateur barber, at least capable of shaving his employer while he is awake, belongs to the realm of Hollywood fantasy. To expect him to do what Kipling's valet did is fantasy cubed, and as I say, every man to whom I have read the relevant passage has agreed that the luxury it describes is closer to being absolutely and utterly unimaginable than any absurd fancy or secret longing which his own sinful mind has ever conceived.

But this is a glimpse of Florence, and I had better relate these musings to life in the cradle of the Renaissance before anybody feels cheated. First of all, there are still a few barbershops left here. Secondly, apart from the usual sightseers, tourists, and what British travel agents call "holiday-makers," the town is crammed to overflowing with students – very rich and rich, young and not so young, but mostly American – who have come here "to study art" (if they went to a private school) or "to learn about art" (if they are pretty girls, as a few of them are). None of these people, as far as I have been able to determine, is aware that the gorgeous truth of which they seek to acquire a traveller's knowledge, as though art were a fact of geography and education a discounted railway pass, is the razor-thin boundary between the expanse of skill, such as that of a nonpareil barber, and the depth of luxury, such as the pleasure of being shaved in bed.

It is a truism tending toward banality that, during the centuries that made Florence what it was, art was craft. The artist's divine gift was but a fanciful way of invoicing the artisan's rare skill, another way of counting the cost of and paying for the frescoed ceiling, the family portrait with the angels, the inlaid commode, the marble putti in the ancestral chapel. Of course this form of accounting is older than the Renaissance, as witness the origin of the word "talent" in the Graeco-Roman monetary unit, but it was here in Florence that the system was properly modernized and streamlined. Here Orcagna, Brunelleschi, Ghiberti, Donatello, Uccello, Gozzoli, Verrochio, Pollaiuolo, Ghirlandaio all started out as apprentice goldsmiths. Here you could get your mistress painted snacking on almond macaroons with the head of John the Baptist in the foreground, and pay with a credit card.

Which brings us round to the equally venerable and corollary truism, this one concerning indulgence, dissolution, and all manner of unspeakable sumptuousness and naked luxury. Take a city of top information-age entrepreneurs with hardly an ethical scruple between them, add innumerable Talentis and Buontalentis in place of the sadly-miniskirted little Ms. Guice, and instead of a snivelling article in a Condé Nast magazine you get one of the longest encyclopaedia entries of Western civilization, from "Santa Maria Novella begun," say, to "Palazzo Uffizi completed." It is obviously true that in those days, even as art was craft, profligacy was aesthetics, more was more, and "simplicity," in the words of the Russian proverb, "worse than theft." Which did not mean, however, that everybody simply got drunk every night and made merry by leafing through pornographic ephemera. For not only isn't luxury necessarily enfeebling, it isn't always a precursor of debauchery. Besides, how surely do the ways of austerity lead to vigour? And how good a safeguard against bestiality is discomfort?

Every great truism can only benefit from a timely and judicious inversion, and it occurs to me that as the American boys and girls arrive in Florence to learn about art, they ought to be told that they are barking up the wrong tree. Because in the closing years of the twentieth century, craft – not art – is art. Painters, poets, playwrights, philosophers are now a dime a dozen, thanks to the universal system of liberal education, while the skills of a professional barber, an accomplished baker, or a distinguished bootblack are now as rare, as valuable, and as imperilled by the scruples of those who would not be known as sybarites as the talents of artists and writers in the darkest, hardest, meanest, least civilized or indulgent ages. Those who have no sympathy for the decline of such skills, and no will whatever to save them through individual acts of patronage at the risk of being themselves considered decadent, can never acquire the knowledge of the genesis and procreation of talent, known as the Renaissance, for which they have come here.

But instead of sympathy, passivity. Instead of absorption, blinkered, slavish diligence. Instead of Florence, a bottle of Coke and three straws. And finally I begin to dream of addressing these bejeaned Savonarolas, these top information-age entrepreneurs of the future, through a megaphone from the Arnolfo Tower down to the Piazza della Signoria. You want to learn about art, boys and girls? Then patronize an expensive barber, for God's sake! Buy an emerald crocodile suit with lapels worked in llama gut dyed to match, have a master furrier make you an opera cloak of orangutan skin trimmed in barguzin sable, have fresh *millefoglie* in bed every morning. Try not to order pizza by the slice! Who knows, perhaps the day will come when somebody suggests that you should get a Gulfstream and you will answer that you've decided to get a valet instead, an old Florentine who is simply the Machiavelli of the straight razor. *That* would show education!

... in Florence "to study art"

XI Florence

Beyond Bugs

I am actually writing this from a lonely place called Marsiliana, in the Maremma region of Tuscany, where my Florentine hosts have a hunting lodge. It is less than half an hour by car from the Argentario coastline, my inspiration for last summer's seaside jottings, and I would drive past its desolate form whenever a group of us got together to go bathing in the hot springs of Saturnia, much further inland. We always used to ask everybody on the way, from ancient, moustachioed somnolent taxi drivers to neat, young, eager petrol station attendants, about the apparently inaccessible town on top of the hill, and were always told that it's not a town, just an old castle whose owners are never there.

Well, now it turns out that it isn't a castle either, just a hunting lodge, and adding to the confusion, not only are the owners, but smarmy old Navrozov is there as well, busily blending in with the scenery in his borrowed Barbour and gum boots. "*Iz gryazi v knyazi,*" as we say in Russian. Literally this means "up from the dirt to mix with princes," but I like the proverb so much I think it may be worthwhile to dramatize it a bit. If I kept a diary in verse, in the style of Pushkin's *Eugene Onegin*, what follows here might be the entry under "Marsiliana":

> In the Maremma, shooting wild boar.
> Now, Ralph Laurens of the world
> And Ronald Lauders:
> Behold a son of Khrushchev's slums
> Hobnobbing with a prince's sons
> And daughters!

I am not sure this is ideal publicity for cashmere turtlenecks, but at any rate it has helped me to work some populist cynicism into the warp and woof of the story from the very beginning, so as not to have to worry later about sounding a little too breathless for my own good. As for Ronald Lauder, he is, believe it or not, a leading collector of mediaeval arms and armour, a kind of Frederick Stibbert of the Hamptons. Really, sometimes I just can't decide whose foibles are funnier and more pitiful, mine or other people's.

Even assuming it is mine, I must boldly proclaim that I hate the countryside in winter, and in Marsiliana I finally realized that this feeling goes far beyond the city dweller's conventional squeamishness, beyond bugs, beyond big fish eating little fish, beyond homosexual intercourse involving two apparently stray mutts committed in broad daylight and observed through a picture window during breakfast. I realized that what I dislike about the countryside most of all is the insidious facsimile of contentment it promises, that smug, saccharine parody of the myriad real satisfactions one experiences in town even when simply crossing the street without being hit by a late-night bus, or sitting down in a café with the hard-earned foreknowledge of a good espresso. Urban life is order, which is conducive to ordered thought. Country life, by contrast, toughens the skin while softening the brain.

Consider the notoriously deleterious effect the country has on otherwise perfectly well-behaved city children who, just hours earlier, could be seen working on chess openings and asking charmingly naive questions about the second part of *Faust*. Yet here they are, those same children, rolling in the dirt with three-legged dogs or brandishing muddy sticks. As for the effect on adults, it is perhaps enough to remark on the self-satisfied air with which grown men light a fire in the grate, or tend a wood-burning stove of the kind apparent in every bedroom in Marsiliana. They really suppose, by defrauding their families into thinking for a few hours that the rooms have central heating, that they have achieved something of lasting ethical value. *Deus misereatur!*

But then of course there is also my frankly hedonist side – which some people might suppose would anyway be wholly dominant in the easy life of a Russian wastrel – and the truth is that nothing alarms this aspect of my character more than the sight of a bare tree in wintertime. A leafless branch sprinkled with freezing rain is, for me, what a barbed-wire fence punctuated with watchtowers is for a person of ordinarily sturdy disposition. "Holy hell," I say to myself, "just give civilization a little push, and the whole world will be covered with trees exactly like that one." In short, dominant or not in the general run of urban existence, in the country my sybaritic side comes to the fore. Here it rears up and protests, it winds up grandfather clocks in dimly lit hallways and ransacks old cupboards for train timetables, it makes friends with excruciatingly boring couples without children who happen to own cars.

When resisted, as good manners and the peculiar responsibilities of a guest dictate it must be, this irrepressible side of me becomes truly vicious. How inventive its sarcasm! How observant its criticisms! How condescending its acknowledgment of life's simpler blessings! Thus, in Marsiliana, it quickly seized upon the C and F for "*Calda*" and "*Fredda*" engraved on the water taps, muttering at bath time that they stood for "Cold" and "Freezing." Later that evening, in the library, just as the Western, resilient rest of me was beginning to thaw out in front of the fire with a dry grappa, a perfectly passable Tuscan cigar, and a volume of Winston Churchill's wartime memoirs, my Eastern, decadent side resumed its suit. With perfect timing, it drew my attention to the description of Sir Winston's stay at State Villa No. 7, near Moscow, in August 1942:

> The hot and cold water gushed. I longed for a hot bath after the journey…. All was instantly prepared. I noticed that the basins were not fed by separate hot and cold water taps and that they had no plugs. Hot and cold turned on at once through a single spout, mingled to exactly the temperature one desired. Moreover, one did not wash one's hands in the basins, but under the flowing current of the taps.

"In a modest way," adds the English country bumpkin with becoming humility, "I have adopted this system at home. If there is no scarcity of water it is far the best." And who might you be, exclaimed my troublesome side driving the point home, to disagree with him? Come on, be fair! Should his wide-eyed fascination with Stalin's state-of-the-art faucets be considered somehow objectionable just because they are Stalin's?

Anyway, in the days when Churchill took the plunge, at State Villa No. 7 and also in Teheran and in Yalta, the hunting estate of Marsiliana had nine thousand hectares. After the war ended, the Communist local authorities expropriated all the arable land and much of the forest, leaving my Florentine hosts with 2700 hectares of hillside underbrush. Back then, hunting wild boar was only a pastime, while real wealth was believed to lie in good fat Maremman land, suitable for agricultural use. Since then the value of such land plummeted – it is now only worth as much as the European Community will pay farmers for not growing anything edible on it – while the useless underbrush, where the wild boar thrives, has become precious. Rich businessmen from all over the world want to hunt there, for the same funny reason they want to wear Ralph Lauren tweeds and collect mediaeval armour.

A few days after I arrived in Marsiliana my hosts were informed by the local authorities, who no longer call themselves Communist, that all hunting permits of the estate are revoked until a substantial tract of the underbrush is legally ceded to them in perpetuity. There was much shouting during lunch, and everyone had the kind of face that people have when something obviously bad yet deeply inexplicable happens to them.

So I took off my borrowed Barbour and gum boots, and thought again that living in the country in wintertime, without mixer taps and all the other creature comforts of city life, softens the brain. Look at Winston Churchill.

... there was much shouting during lunch

XII Florence

Leonardo's Flying Machine

These are probably my last days in Florence, and I must say that it is with somewhat mixed feelings that I turn my back on the treasury of the Renaissance. Oh, sure, I tried to like living here. I tried it the way the French writer André Gide tried to like living in Stalin's Moscow, reasonably confident that he would not have to live there forever, but none the less winding up his stay with a dirty rotten slanderous exposé. In his case, if memory serves, revelation came at the sight of a fellow's badly mangled fingers which, he suddenly realized, had been crushed in the vice of doctrine. In my case, it was the umpteenth glimpse, in a souvenir shop window, of Leonardo's flying machine, coupled with the sudden realization that the damn thing didn't fly.

Is there anyone out there who has not, at one time or another in the course of a wretched life poisoned by Enlightenment myths, looked with cowardly reverence at that absurd drawing? Medici's Florence and Stalin's Moscow have much in common. Both were designed for propaganda purposes, and each in its own way retains the power to intimidate the sceptic. It has taken me several months to see that the silly contraption didn't fly, never flew, and would probably be more likely to fly if it were designed by a lunatic on the run from a mental asylum, by a marauding Romanian soldier the morning after he pilfered his way through a substantial wine cellar, by Fred Flintstone in one of his less practical moods. And the catapult! At least Stalin's weapons were the best of their kind, while Leonardo's catapult would not hurt a Luccan fly, and not because of how big 'em flies grow out there in Lucca. Yet every gift shop in Florence can offer you, at the price of about two hundred United States dollars, a miniature replica of this pacifist dream made of handsomely varnished mahogany.

At first I reasoned away the awkward realization the way one usually reasons away such realizations, by analogy. If Uccello's *Rout of San Romano*, say, or Michelangelo's *David*, were the equivalents of IS-8 (the heavy tank "Iosif Stalin," later known as T-10) or of a MiG (the fighter designed for Stalin by Mikoyan and Gurevich), then the flying machine and the catapult were something like Stalinist architecture, or the gigantic effigy of *The Worker and the Peasant Woman* at the Exposition of the Achievements of People's Industry in Moscow. While I was reading the technical specifications of the T-10, in a *History Today* chart comparing it with the main tanks of the West, the analogy held. But then, looking at the David, with its bovine neck, its outsize hands, and its spirit of arrogant hyper-realism, it occurred to me that this humanist masterpiece was too literally like *The Worker and the Peasant Woman* for the analogy to support itself. And straight away all around me the past of Florence began crashing into the world's present, in a scene from a Hollywood movie about Atlantis starring Kirk Douglas and a volcano of bosomy blondes.

Modern propaganda is a lot like modern art, in the sense that both sell dysfunctional versions of ordinary things, including food and clothing, to a culturally intimidated audience that never dares to ask why the representation is not labelled accordingly. If you see an electric iron that irons shirts, this is an iron; if you see an electric iron that does not iron shirts (especially when it is one thousand feet high and stands in front of an office building with an address like 1000 Federal Plaza), this is a work of contemporary sculpture. Similarly, liberty is often a good thing, equality has its uses, and in the context of Christian morality a place for fraternity can obviously be found; but "liberty, equality, fraternity" is political propaganda designed to deceive, to mislead, and to hide the reality of broken fingers from visiting Frenchmen. There was an old Soviet joke about a shopper who, upon seeing a generous length of cardboard tube representing "Hunter's Sausage" in the shop window, asks for a kilo and is told that this is the display. "No Hunter's? All right, I'll take a kilo of display," he murmurs with habitual resignation. The point is that it was in Medici's Florence that modern propaganda was born.

It had to have been born here because, although in name a republic since 1293, by the middle of the fifteenth century Florence was being ruled by Cosimo de' Medici, and after his death by his son and grandson, as by "a King in all but name." This name business is at the very heart of the matter. Thus one notes that the Tornabuoni, Florentine grandees who gave their daughter Lucrezia in marriage to Cosimo's son and dynastic successor Piero, had changed their name from the noble Tornaquinci, having so altered their coat of arms as "to evade the disadvantages attaching to their birth." In other words, the indecorous chasm between reality and appearance, in a place where noblemen had to change names and renounce their aristocratic past before being eligible for participation in public life, had to be camouflaged, and camouflaged well. It was republican art that introduced perspective into painting, and made verisimilitude its aesthetic aim. And it was republican politics that produced political propaganda as the panacea for the ills of oligarchic dictatorship.

The parallel between the "master of the country," as Aeneas Silvius de' Piccolomini, later Pope Pius II, alternatively called him, and Stalin goes well beyond Cosimo's legendary self-effacing modesty (he held office for a total of ninety days during his thirty years in power) and his famously acerbic, indeed rather Caucasian, sense of humour (asked to introduce a law forbidding priests to gamble, he said that it would be better to begin by forbidding them loaded dice), both necessary qualities for coming to power, as they both did, through the imperceptibly gradual subordination of an existing political *apparat*. There is their total unscrupulousness, in all things great and small: Stalin, a Great Russian Chauvinist of his own making, entrusted the design of his fighter plane to the team of an Armenian and a Jew, while Cosimo, who piously "emblazoned even the monks' privies" with his heraldic balls, did not hesitate to embrace the "whoremonger and scrounger" Fra Filippo Lippi. There is the Molotov-Ribbentrop Pact with the bastard condottiere Francesco Sforza, whom Cosimo had shrewdly fostered long before his takeover of Milan was consummated in the marriage to Bianca Visconti, just as Stalin had secretly supported the National Socialists over the Communists in Weimar Germany. There is even Molotov himself, in the figure of Cosimo's sidekick Puccio Pucci, and if one looks hard enough one can just make out Trotsky in the "tiresome, vain and cantankerous" agitator, partisan of the exiled Albizzi, Francesco Filelfo.

But the main key to the parallel is found in the power of the legitimized lie which Florence's

Pater Patriae and our own Father of the Peoples have created, and perpetuated, in their epoch-specific, yet kindred, ways. The constitutional reforms framed by Pucci in the wake of the rout of the Albizzi in 1434, were, like Stalin's Constitution, a gateway to the new era of virtual tyranny disguised as virtual democracy. According to a historian of the period,

> the *Grandi* were now all declared *Popolani* which gratified the nobles, who were thus theoretically rendered eligible for election to office, while pleasing the *popolo minuto* who chose to interpret the measure as commendably democratic. The people were given greater satisfaction when it was seen that the most talented amongst them, despite their humble origins, were now considered, for the first time in the history of Florence, worthy of holding official positions in the State.

Stalin's Constitution, it must be borne in mind, allowed for ballot-boxes to be delivered to the bedside of the sick on election day. And yet, the historian continues,

> of the 159 newly qualified citizens from the Santa Maria Novella quarter whose names were placed in the *borse* in 1453, no less than 145 were sons, grandsons or brothers of men who had been considered eligible for office in 1449.

In other words, what the Italians would these days call *una grossa fregatura*. A great swindle, which required great art to cover it up. And, great art aside, from here to the restructured new democratic Russia – or, if you prefer, to the American bumper stickers that read I LOVE MY NATION BUT FEAR MY GOVERNMENT – it is but a short step.

And so I confess that as I leave Florence, this treasury-of-wow-the-Renaissance to which I bid farewell seems almost a part of my childhood, not unlike the enclave of Stalin's writers and artists where I was raised. Yet these grandiose monuments to the sleight of hand known since the days of the Medici as modern democracy are now at the heart of world culture. Can one really ever leave Florence, any more than Gide could leave Stalin's Moscow?

…all around me the past of Florence began crashing into the world's present

XIII Florence

The Chic and the Psychic

I already sounded the alarm. This really is an impossible city to get out of. And so, having bid my farewells, I'm still here, despite the fact that the rent has been paid in advance on a perfectly adequate little eyrie over the Grand Canal in Venice. The place even has a spacious terrace overlooking the charred remains of the Fenice, where, whenever I grow tired of looking at the perennially idle construction cranes paid for by the friends of opera everywhere, my future impressions of Italy will effloresce like damp brick. If ever I get myself onto this spacious terrace of mine, that is.

The hereditary proprietor of the Venetian palazzo, Baron F—, turned out to be a cousin of a friend of mine from Cambridge, which was discovered quite by chance while the estate agent was showing me round the vacant apartment. So we immediately sat down to some suitably laconic, crystalline white from the Veneto, and by and by the sparse conversation turned to Florence and her ways. When I told him where I was staying, an ominous shadow crossed his brow. "You will not be here before spring, my friend," he said. "I can take your money now if you like, but you will not be here in time for Carnival. I know Florence, and I know these people. They will not let you go when you want to leave. They want to decide everything."

I murmured something by way of polite disbelief. What exactly was he talking about? Voodoo? Brainwashing? Hypnotic influence? "More like telepathy," he replied, unsmiling. "You'll see. When the crunch comes, you'll find out that they can read your mind." Gradually the subject petered out, and by the time we sat down to lunch at the smallest and cosiest of the five small cosy tables at Ernesto Ballarin's Da Arturo, where my compatriot Nureyev had left a lasting cultural imprint by teaching the owner to fry potatoes and mushrooms together in the Russian manner, the conversation was about food, tax evasion, and the Venetian way of doing things.

This Venetian way of doing things I like very much, by the way, because basically it involves not doing them. Every man here is a careful dresser, a dapper and exceedingly complex arrangement of tasteful checks, stripes, and dots that cannot but make the onlooker whistle, thinking something like boy oh boy, if this fellow has so much energy to spare before he leaves the house in the morning, think of how much he has left over for the rest of the day! In fact, this is almost entirely deceptive, because all of the fellow's energy, all his life force as it were, has in fact gone into achieving that sartorially precarious equilibrium between corporeality and imagination, and what little is left is the strength to raise an *ombra* to the mouth without spilling some Cabernet on the tablecloth in a feeble and indecorous lapse. I know I'm going to do well in Venice. Being gloriously one-eyed in a land of the blind is my idea of belonging. And if they denounce me as a grasping overachiever, so be it.

The other day, in a book about Voltaire I was reading, I found some references to a Venetian named Algarotti who came to stay at Cirey, the Champagne estate where the great controversialist spent half his life shacking up with Mme. du Châtelet. Carlyle once described him as "not supremely beautiful, though much the gentleman in manners as in ruffles and ingeniously logical; rather yellow in mind as in skin and with a taint of obsolete Venetian macassar," which, after a day spent in male company in Venice, sounded just about right to me. Still, I was curious about Signor Algarotti's contribution to the world of ideas, which must have served as his pass-key to Cirey. It turned out that this was a book entitled *Newtonianismo per le dame*, "a simplification of Newton's theories intended for Italian women."

Anyway, when I got back to Florence that evening I had every intention of telling Princess C— that, wonderful as life had been in her famous city, in her historic house and under her illustrious family's protection, I could no longer afford to pay what it cost. And what it cost, incidentally, I no longer have any fear of revealing, for the simple reason that whenever a pretentious foreigner rents something fancy in Italy, it always costs the same number of millions. I need not convert this number into dollars or sterling, or explain what it includes, or even mention whether it is due weekly, monthly, or annually. The figure, predictable as a Henry James formula for romantic disillusionment, is a symbolic compact which represents the new-world tenant's naivety on the one hand and, on the other, the old-world landlord's legitimate desire to protect ancient relics from being overrun by hordes of visitors who are no less tightfisted for being so very naive. Hence, whether you rent a seaside villa in a fashionable resort, or the most architecturally important house in a provincial town, or a floor of a notable palazzo in a large city, the price will always be the same and you will always have to pay it in cash.

The landlady was waiting up for me. If I were telling the story of a poor student lodging in a cheap boarding house, this would be the way to crank up the melodrama, but since mine is more the story of a rake's progress, I will say instead that the princess asked me to tea. "I *think* you are thinking of moving," she said, doing absolutely nothing to obscure the emphasis of the remark, which fell rather more heavily on her own thinking than on mine. I gulped some tea, recalling Baron F—'s warning about psychic Florentines of just a few hours earlier. "I know we've agreed a certain figure, which you've been paying," she went on, knowing only too well that I was already three weeks late with the month's rent, "but now that I realize you're thinking of leaving Florence, how would it strike you if I told you that I only wanted half?"

Spooky, that's how, is what I remember actually thinking, though at this juncture the princess chose not to read my mind and anyway the thought did not linger. "After all, when we first met I did not know you." Convincing, perfectly convincing, I suddenly said to myself, as if waking from some ugly confrontational dream and now beginning to imagine all the good uses to which I could put the rubber-banded wad, called "cutlet" in New Russian parlance, when next one found its way into my pocket. These Florentines are nothing if not perfectly convincing. The princess does have a charming smile. Now that she knows me fifty percent better than before, the rent is halved. Convincing! And the tea is quite good, incidentally. Assam?

"Ceylon. So that's settled, then," she summed up brightly. "You're staying."

It remains for me to add that during the two months that followed our conversation certain changes came into the tenant's life at the Palazzo C—. The wood for the fireplaces was not as dry and no longer brought up with the same enthusiasm as before. The other chambermaid, not wonderfully obedient Lucia, came more often and inaugurated the noxious practice of presenting household bills for such trifling items as candles and cayenne pepper. The choir practice in the other wing became less tuneful, and seemed louder and more intrusive. Finally and most significantly, I was being charged for heating, electricity, gas, and the rest of life's prose, with the result that now, after the sums have been done, I can only wince and tell myself the terrible truth, which is that as a matter of practical reality my rent never changed. The same symbolic number of millions as always was actually withdrawn from my pocket, this time by means of an accounting procedure that I can describe as telekinetic.

But as Baron F— had foretold, the important thing as far as Princess C— was concerned was that she got us to change our plans. ("Plans?! What plans can a lazy Venetian make with a drunk Muscovite?! *Per piacere, sii serio!*" is what I would probably hear if I could read her mind.) I am now leaving Florence not on my schedule, and less on his, but on the whim of a descendant of those shrewd merchant bankers who dealt in the absurd gullibility of mankind for so long that the manipulative cynicism in their blood can pass, in the sleepy, sleepier eyes of the rest of us frivolous and indolent Venetians, for a bit of spooky hypnosis.

...I know I'm going to do well in Venice

XIV Venice

First Impressions

It has only been a few weeks since I used my tears to moisten the mixed-fruit *schiacciata* cake of Florentine captivity, but from the chaise longue on my terrace it seems that this was in another life. Here at last I am at one with my destiny, a spark of cosmic indolence fortuitously restored to the serene plenitude of the great green lagoon, or, in a less overtly Gnostic idiom and the more popular style of Dean Martin and Jerry Lewis,

> First I movèd all my stuff-a
> With a big motoscafo.

No, let me see if I can do better than that:

> Then I placèd each bundle-a
> In a nice old gondola.

And so on. When it comes to first impressions of Venice, obviously the important thing is to stem the creeping sentimentalism associated with the otherwise perfectly reputable soundtrack of a certain homosexual cult movie based on a lugubrious German novella, and now that that's been pretty much achieved I can be serious.

Sleeping in Venice is like no other sleeping I've ever done. This is significant, because since my university days I've done more kinds of sleeping than most people at Yale have read dull books. "No, not more than Harold Bloom!" I hear you cry. Yes, even than Harold Bloom. My approach is likewise characterized by total commitment, which in this case mandates the ownership of some reasonably voluptuous linen, and even a kind of Talmudist frenzy that seizes me whenever it is time to turn off the bedside lamp. Sleeping, for me, is more than the wise man's reading. It is the poor man's gambling.

Venice, meaning its 67,000 native inhabitants and roughly as many naturalized or resident aliens like myself, goes to bed early. By eleven o'clock, eleven-thirty at the latest, the Venetians who have been out for the evening are making their way home, and only the tourists still overhang the canals and crowd the streets in giant, amorphous, apparently purposeless clusters of transient bodies and foreign vocables. There are nine million of *them*, annually. By midnight, when the cafes along the Via della Pace in Rome would just begin doing their shady business, willowy youths winking determinedly at the waiters in the hope of grabbing a white wire-mesh seat near the moving throng, here, and I hesitate to say it for fear of being accused of only having seen Venice in my dreams, yet it is true, by midnight all one hears is the occasional sound of water splashing against wooden piles and mossy stone.

In the daylight the piles, called *bricole* in the Venetian dialect, look like giant stalks of white asparagus. Some are very old. The streets are paved with identical *masegni*, flagstones excised from the volcanic hills of nearby Padua since the time of its annexation to the Republic. But the only sort of stone used in building here, apart from Roman brick, is *pietra d'Istria*. There is a reason for this, as only three kinds of material – wood, combination red-and-yellow clay brick, and just this type of stone quarried in what is now part of Croatia – can withstand prolonged exposure to the elements in the primordial soup in which the city steams like a piece of toast in freshly made bouillabaisse. Iron, whether in oar locks or window latches, has a life expectancy of five years, untreated marble may last a generation, granite awhile longer. The very climate which is Venice, in short, is a kind of subconscious release from individual responsibility, where all constructive striving within the elemental pool of life is ultimately useless and all human effort is doomed, dissolving in due course into the rust and algae of the ages. That suits me fine, and a fresh graffito in Campo S. Stefano confirms that the indigenous attitude to life is conducive to sound ratiocination: "USA Assassins," it reads, "Milosevič Butcher."

By the Rialto I saw some young soldiers in uniform, native Venetians on leave from their unit, chitchatting in dialect with their gondolier friends. I asked them, in my best foreigner's Italian, for some views of the war, which, after all, is being waged as I write from airbases an hour's drive from Mestre, and not exactly under a dense veil of international secrecy. "*Boh!*" they replied cheerfully, in *their* best foreigner's Italian, giving me to understand that they neither knew nor cared. Of what relevance is a world war if a gondola across the Grand Canal is still less than a thousand lire? Of what permanence is peace if the noblest marble will melt like a sugar cube in a cup of tea? Driving wooden *bricole* into the soggy primeval silt, on the other hand – although likewise not of eternal significance – is an undertaking considerably less frivolous. A single one of these trammels of free movement, an ordinary tree trunk about nine metres long, may cost over $2000 to put up, as the right to perform such work is held exclusively, and in such perpetuity as there can be on this impermanent earth, by the professional association of gondoliers.

And then there is the central issue of lunch, which furnishes a further illustration of the city's collective idea of order, justice, and fair play. At the world-famous Harry's Bar or any other restaurant of average distinction, a seafood risotto and some grilled fish, with local Veneto white, will cost the foreigner $150, or $200 if he unnecessarily upsets the impeccably disciplined staff by wearing his baseball cap backwards. But if a Venetian is one of his party, not necessarily acting as host or paying, but merely present at table, the bill will not come to more than $50 a head. This is no urban myth I am passing on here, nor an open secret of the gossipy kind one finds in youth travel guides; it's just the way it is, unapologetic and public as the nose on Dante's face. A fool might call it unfair, and discrimination; but if fools had their way, there would be no good restaurants left in Venice. The moral is that fairness is but an ingredient of happiness, and its obsessive pursuit is as odd as a plateful of cummin, or a tub of lard, for the main course.

Venetians do not seize the day. They prolong it, believing that a good man ought to live as the great city does, sinking beautifully and as slowly as can possibly be arranged. A complex web of apparently intractable urban traditions, ruthlessly syndicalist superstitions, and openly arcane practices of every description, which covers everything from the flavouring of sweetmeats to the mooring of boats, is actually an intricate and effective safety precaution, many centuries in the making, designed to retard the processes of physical corrosion and social erosion. I hope it will not sound too nostalgic if I say that a mere century ago my native country still had a few of these retardant structures in place, and that similar barriers in the United States were forcibly dismantled not very long after. Certainly I have seen with my own eyes, within the last decade, how the wholesale removal of arbitrary and arcane bulwarks against progress – in the name of fairness, social mobility, and untrammelled trade in dogmeat-and-soybean hamburgers – has made England not England.

It is equally sad to reflect that so much of Italy is to suffer the same streamlined fate. It is not specifically the spectre of a European superstate, or the pursuit of American pseudo-prosperity, or the new dream of freedom sold by the telecommunications industry as cunningly as General Motors sold the old one, that are razing the last love of my life to the ground. It is simply the realization, on the part of most decent, working, normal people – in Italy as elsewhere – that things are going in a certain very obvious way, and that one must in the end be a stubborn, recalcitrant, almost suicidally lackadaisical sort of person not to go with the flow.

Well, Venice has not gone with the flow. It has stood athwart it, quite literally, for a thousand years, thanks to the obstinate, insular, suicidally lackadaisical race that inhabits this vividly surreal Canaletto landscape, ever mindful that progress – in any and every sense – is another word for inundation, deluge, entropy, collapse of everything that is truly valuable, really important, and should be preserved just a little longer, and then a little while longer again. While the Superstate of Europe is being mooted, Italy as a whole will doubtless survive the longest among nations as the place with the stamina, or the contrariness, or the capriciousness, or the laziness, or the serenity to deny the Great Khan his spiritual obeisance. And when that Superstate is truly upon us, this Sheherezade of a city will become Superitaly, or Italy's Italy, still lingering as an authentic social organism even as its more worldly, energetic, and accommodating neighbours gorge themselves on artificially inseminated spaghetti from Frankfurt and genetically modified sea bream from Minsk.

Two years ago I wrote in this diary that Italy was where I hoped to make my last stand, or at any rate to have my last sleep. Now I think I know exactly where in Italy.

... still had such retardant measures in place

XV Venice

The Road to "Il Wellness"

The other day I remembered how the Lebanese, by far the most wistfully European of all the social sets in London, used to play an after-dinner parlour game in which the guests won points by boasting of their innocence. For example, if a guest said "I've never been on a private plane," or "I've never tasted Yquem," and everybody else in the room had, he won a point. He lost the point if just one other person present could make the same declaration, whereupon it would be somebody else's turn to try and brag in reverse. The skill of the game is to appraise one's competition, since in a roomful of Sardinian peasants one is unlikely to win a point by claiming never to have been aboard a Meridiana turboprop creaking to Rome, to say nothing of a private jet bound for the Bahamas. "I've never eaten sheep cheese with live maggots" or "I've never seen *Beautiful* on television" would be a much likelier bet in that case. The beauty of the game is its aristocratic, poker-faced egalitarianism: "I've never been on a commercial flight" can net the clever participant a point among playboys as well as among shopkeepers.

But the other big reason I liked the game was because I always won, what with not having gone to school, not having done drugs, not having been to the Bahamas, not having cheated on my wife, not having seen a basketball game, and so on. Still, there were some dinner parties with very stiff competition – young educated people with houses in the South of France who had never visited Naples, intelligent urbane men who had never tasted pork, beautiful women who were not married – and it was then that I would reach for the ace up my sleeve. "I've never been to the gym," I would say, staring blankly into the middle distance just above my hostess's head, and in all my years in London this never lost me a point. Now I can no longer say it. I've *joined* a gym. Yes, here in Venice.

When I rang up a friend in London to share this news, he had me describe in precise detail everything I had seen inside the building. I only realized that he had thought I was lying when he asked me point blank if the purpose of my preposterous confession was to conjure up some sort of atmosphere of moral renewal as an ingenious prelude to borrowing money from him. I suppose he was half expecting that when pressed I would mix genres and tell him that inside the gym I had joined were exercise tables covered with green baize, special machines that spun ivory balls, and fitness instructors with voices like angels and words of encouragement like "twenty-six thirty-two, neighbours by two hundred, gentleman in the back." It was only when I used such place-specific terms as "stair master" and "treadmill," adding that I had drunk no more than two bottles of ordinary table wine during the last three days and was actually thinking of quitting smoking, that he let go of his scepticism and began to wonder in earnest if the gentleman in the back had gone soft in the head. Well, the truth of the matter is that I have, and Venice is to blame.

… the very topography of this strange town

Of course Venice has a big reputation when it comes to decadence. The reason for this is that most punters who have been chewed up and spat out by this town during the last couple of centuries believed themselves to be in a state of grace when they first arrived, with the consequence that the ambiguities of Venice sooner or later made mincemeat out of their vain delusion. Equally, if you believe yourself to be a rake or a rogue to the marrow of your bones the moment you first feel the tender undulation of a gondola beneath your feet after a lifetime of what you never thought was particularly steady ground, then the salutary effect of Venice can only be compared to the wheatgrass juice prescribed at the Optimum Health Institute of San Diego to patients whose maladies do not yield to conventional medicine, except that this treatment really works. In other words, Venice does not corrupt. It merely transmutes virtue into vice, and vice versa.

The secret of its success lies in its shameless, chaste ambivalence, of the kind that would permit the most disinterested of observers to use the word "chaste" as a synonym for "shameless" in the description, for instance, of a young girl trying on her first string of pearls with only a cheval glass for company. The very topography, and the toponymy, of this strange town ought to provide the unprejudiced visitor with plenty of examples on his first day here. If one wishes to go from a certain place to another, one can always get there by water; or one always can get there by land, keeping in mind that some of the canals one takes were once land; while some of the streets were once water. The back of the palazzo where I live faces a street called Salizada della Chiesa o del Teatro. This means that the street used to be a canal; and that some people thought it led to the church while others thought it led to the theatre.

Just across a canal from where I am runs Calle Corner Piscopia o Loredan, which some people thought had just one notable family in residence, while others obviously disagreed. There are seven streets here, admittedly in different parts of town, all called Calle della Chiesa. In fact, there are four different streets in Venice called Calle del Angelo, three Calle Bembo, seven Calle del Cristo, three Calle del Dose, and so on across the map and down the alphabet until one gets to the two Calle Zorzi, one in San Marco and the other in Castello. Typically, each of the 441 bridges spanning the tiny canals will have displayed on its side the heraldic markings of the two or three families who jointly built it, a deliberate precaution ensuring that none of the bridges would have exclusive proprietary associations; in this, as in everything they do, Venetians have shown that they abhor the notion of the pontifex, who might give to a place its proper name and to all life a single definition.

More than a hint of polytheistic paganism is in the air at the conjunction of treeless, salty earth and cloudy Siberian emerald-coloured water, of Turkish fatalism and indigenous languor, of Gallic sophistication and northern brawn. This troubles my friend and landlord, a Venetian to his fingertips of whom more will be said later, Baron F—. At Easter I brought him along to hear the midnight mass at the Greek church here, this being his first time ever in an Orthodox cathedral, and he later confessed that he was unable to sleep the rest of the night. Only in the atmosphere of total ambivalence that is Venice, it seems, can a man in his fifties, with an important social position, a young wife, and small children, worry about religion the way people elsewhere – in parts of the world more professedly moral or wholeheartedly Christian – worry about their business affairs, falling interest rates, and the price of the U.S. dollar.

"But tell me," he kept repeating, "is Mussorgsky's music really Christian? We know that Wagner, who is the West's Mussorgsky, was a paganist. Are the Russians and the Greeks really different? Can your people, unlike ourselves in the rest of the Christian world, combine pleasure with goodness, wisdom with contradiction, polyphony with morality?" I answered him in the usual way men do when embarrassingly emotional questions are put to them, obfuscating rather than clarifying the points at issue, but within a few days I was out there on the Zattere embankment, filling out membership forms at the Palestra Club Delfino. "*La Strada verso il Wellness,*" proclaimed the poster adorned with a line drawing of the ecologically problematic sea animal of the whale order.

Only a week before I would have said nuke 'em. But now the gentleman in the back only looked meekly all around him, as though saying good-bye to his troubled past, and reflected that the annual cost of living this new dolphin life, in this improbable and contradictory town, is much less than the cost of losing just one of his favourite neighbour bets in the time it takes to light a cigarette or mutter a swearword.

XVI Venice

Guilt by Association

Reading over my first impressions of Venice I spot the word "improbable," which has somehow slipped in through the barbed-wire fence of watchful obstinacy I have been building up in order to keep all manner of breathless tripe out of these periodic jottings. I am sorry, and promise that nothing of the kind will ever happen again. Never again, in the fortified, hermetic space that is this diary, will anybody come across anything that will so much as suggest, for example, that

> Everything that happens in Venice has this inherent improbability, of which the gondola, floating, insubstantial, at once romantic and haunting, charming and absurd, is the symbol.

Come to think of it, what I am in a position to offer here is a whole list of specific promises, which may at first sound difficult to fulfill but I regard as binding. I promise not to exploit the simile of *trompe-l'oeil* when speaking of "this painted deception," meaning Venice. I undertake never to allude to the "friend of Byron's, the Countess Querini-Benzoni, *la biondina in gondoleta*." And of course I will make no reference whatever to the story of the city's founding, apocryphal or not, by refugees from Attila the Hun:

> Refugees, fleeing from him on the mainland, sought safety on the fishing islets and began to build their improbable city, houses of wattles and twigs set on piles driven into the mud, "like sea-birds' nests," wrote Cassiodorus.

Equally off limits will be the city's "eternal present," together with its alleged function as "part museum, part amusement park," and the contention that "the tourist Venice *is* Venice: the gondolas, the sunsets, the changing light, Florian's, Quadri's, Torcello, Harry's Bar, Murano, Burano, the pigeons, the glass beads, the vaporetto. Venice is a folding picture post-card of itself." More uncompromising still will be the pitiless curtaining off of all mirrors, and possibly of all other reflective surfaces, rather in the manner of the childbirth scene in *War and Peace*. Without such apparently superstitious precautions, the unwary reader might be led to believe that

> It is all for the ear and the eye, this city, but primarily for the eye. Built on water, it is an endless succession of reflections and echoes, a mirroring.

And, final and most important, in the months to come the hoariest platitude of all will be laid bare and obliterated, in this space as in civilized modern minds, this being the view that "*nothing can be said here* (including this statement) *that has not been said before.*"

This view, with its parenthetical nod to Henry James, as well as every single one of the improbable – the only word for it, really – banalities just cited, is drawn from Mary McCarthy's slim and influential volume of cultural reportage, which the *New Yorker* first serialized some forty years ago, *Venice Observed*. When Count V—, a kind neighbour possessed of an inquiring mind and an admirable cook, asked my opinion of the little paperback edition he had lent me, I answered that despite the recent Hiss revelations there were some forms of McCarthyism I still found deplorable. Stupid Russian joke, I know, but at least the celebrated authoress would have been offended.

Anyway, here is how the celebrated authoress elaborates that last point, about the utter futility of gazing into Venice's "mirror held up to its own shimmering image":

> One gives up the struggle and submits to a classic experience. One accepts the fact that what one is about to feel or say has not only been said before by Goethe or Musset but is on the tip of the tongue of the tourist from Iowa who is alighting in the Piazzetta with his wife in her furpiece and jewelled pin. Those Others, the existential enemy, are here identical with oneself. After a time in Venice, one comes to look with pity on the efforts of the newcomer to disassociate himself from the crowd.

Note the unmistakable touch of McCarthyism, so instinctively felt by us Russians. From the cowardly safety of the grave she now tries to tar me with the same brush she has used on that honest and probably not at all loquacious Iowan. She goes on:

> He has found a "little" church – has he? – quite off the beaten track, a real gem, with inlaid colored marbles on a soft dove grey, like a jewel box. He means Santa Maria dei Miracoli. As you name it, his face falls. It is so well known, then?

Not to me, lady. We're all rednecks here, for once.

Quite apart from the colossal snootiness – and of the cheapest, bath-and-racquets kind, of course – inherent in this approach to a place of whose very language, after all, this American observer is conspicuously ignorant, what is culturally catastrophic about it is the inevitable companion of country-club snobbery: guide-book materialism. Indeed, much of the argument consists of a thinly veiled register of the pictures and architectural monuments visited, so that, by implication, the reader can draw the conclusion that once he too has seen all there is to see, there will be, logically, no need to stay. To want to stay is to want to dissociate oneself from the crowd, which is at once futile and pitiful. To want to stay is to want to leave New York.

Last week, as it happens, I had to attend the wedding of an American couple held at great expense at the old Rothschild stronghold of Ferrières, near Paris. There were 320 guests, for the most part young, rich New Yorkers. One exception was a twenty-year-old Italian, whom I overheard asking the mother of the bride if the château had belonged to her family. Why no, she said, I thought a little too dreamily. Then to the bridegroom's family, he guessed again, helpfully.

No, she said, this time a little more firmly. The boy from Treviso thought about her answer for a while, as if wondering whether saying anything else on the subject might not seem impertinent, but curiosity got the better of him. Then why are you having the wedding here, he asked.

You see, it's the material infrastructure that counts, I wanted to shout to him. It's a kind of all-the-madeleine-you-can-eat restaurant they're running over there, don't you understand? An all-the-allusions-you-can-find lending library. Rent the château, check out the church, recognize the painting – these *are* the associations. Anything else is an endless succession of reflections and echoes, a shimmering mirroring and all that.

During cocktails, on a famous lawn bounded by a famous lake, I spoke with no fewer than a third of the New York contingent, mostly – like the Italian – out of plain conversational curiosity, as well as the customary obligation to mingle. Everyone I spoke to was expensively dressed, even beautiful, perfectly behaved, and worked for an American investment bank. But by the end of the second minute of conversation, which, I eventually realized, was the moment they discovered that I live (*live?*) in Venice (*Venice, Italy?*), each of these bright young things in succession turned on his or her heels and walked away without so much as a pitying glance.

Now fairly desperate, I tried London as a plausible residence and this got me to the third minute, no more. I then tried saying that my parents live in New York, that my wife has an American passport, that I am practically related to the bride, that I promise to name my next child Washington, "DC for short," and so on. Useless, pathetic, immature! A salesman of insubstantial, shimmering associations! We've heard it all before! Venice, Italy! He says he lives there!

> No stones are so trite as those of Venice, that is, precisely, so well worn. It has
> been part museum, part amusement park, living off the entrance fees of tourists,
> ever since the eighteenth century, when its former sources of revenue ran dry.

This I could read in their unamused eyes. Mind you, I had been drinking like a born Venetian, and was hustled off to dinner before one of these conversational engagements had time to turn into a drunken brawl, so perhaps I was just imagining things.

But anyway, I think this tale is a pretty good folding picture postcard of itself, as a tale of Venice should be. Are you happy, Mary McCarthy?

… are you happy, Mary McCarthy?

XVII Apulia

At the End of Italy

I am writing this from a cottage near Santa Maria di Leuca, on the southernmost tip of Italy in the Adriatic. As the luggage, containing my maps and guidebooks, arrived only yesterday, I cannot really be expected to say anything worth believing about the land or its people. But this morning I breakfasted on perfectly ripe damson plums overhanging the stone table on the patio, and the coffee was good. In a way, knowing myself as well as I do, it is already pretty clear what the next few weeks will be like.

I was in London in June and early July, roughly from Ascot to Wimbledon, all keyed up, as the flower girl says in the movie, from that famous pink concoction of fine weather, predatory women, and grinning men in grey still known as the Season. One scene in particular, in the dining room of Aspinalls, is vivid in my mind, and I would like to relive it now, against a background of furiously independent-minded bees and reedy echoes of southern voices that sound as one imagines Homeric antiquity. I was eavesdropping on a table of four Italian men from Milan and two English businessmen with Estuary accents, all in their late fifties, when a gargantuan platter of lightly poached wild salmon trout made its appearance and the conversation, which had been tending to food anyway, suddenly burst the banks and turned raucous. *Ah, salmone! No, trota!*

Before I invite the reader to laugh out loud as I laughed just then, I had better explain something. While I am prepared to accept as given that a hundred years ago food in London was as good as anywhere in Europe, it is equally true that the generation now living was brought up on overcooked broccoli, bacon grease, and fine claret, by which they meant mediocre Bordeaux. I used to find their innocence wholly admirable, on the grounds that it is always easier to find a good roast chicken and a glass of drinkable red than an interesting person to talk to or a friend who won't make a pass at your wife; in fact, I would admit that I associated their innocence with moral rectitude, if not downright saintliness. "Don't you know there's a war on?" their menus seemed to say, and since as far as I was concerned indeed there was, I always nodded politely and had the broccoli.

Meanwhile, of course, the flower girl was busy loosening all the social screws. Thalassotherapy and *balayage* became the new bywords for success. New restaurants appeared every day, cappuccino frothed on every street corner in Chelsea, specialty shops sold exotic Basque cheeses, obscure Piedmont hams, and allegedly Apulian *burrate*, until finally the once-upright London has come to stand on its head like a kind of junior-league Manhattan. This means that instead of two or three coffee bars where in the old days you couldn't get an espresso, there are now two or three hundred espresso bars where you can't get an espresso. Instead of having your broccoli overcooked, you never get broccoli at all and have to feed on Malaysian baby dwarf fig leaves, or some other such cowardly thing. And if you mention the war, people think you are bonkers.

The effect of all this on the Londoner's psyche has been one of massive confusion, something along the lines of the cult television series *The Prisoner*. They no longer know where they are, who is making them drink cappuccino and why, where the husband's secretary finds the money to buy strappy ostrich sandals, who paid for the nanny's holiday in the Maldives, or why *The Times* is always going on about the Internet while the BBC is forever breaking the taboo of lesbian love. Now imagine. Into this unsightly mess, which is the present-day, Manhattanized, dazed London, walk four middle-aged Italian men in dark-blue Caraceni suits and shirts from Siniscalchi. And ogle the lightly poached salmon trout as if God had put it there for them.

Admittedly, Aspinalls – now as ten or fifteen years ago, before my fair lady's revolution ended, as revolutions do, with the social *reductio ad absurdum* – has the best restaurant in England, in part because it is subsidized by the gambling and in part because John Aspinall is an old-fashioned eccentric who has some of the produce organically grown on his own farm. All the puddings are made in his house by his own pastry chef and then delivered to the club by his own driver. But what's so poignantly absurd about the scene I'm describing is that the Milanese visitors were taking it all for granted, assuming that they had been brought to Aspinalls for a taste of the new London, the international one, the one without social barriers and overcooked veg.

Soon their excited conversation took a familiar course, as they argued over the translation of "grouse" into Italian. If this is indeed the new international London, I reflected, and if what they want to talk about is plain old food, then this conversation ought to go very differently. Why not begin by asking each other simple questions like "How do you say 'fresh tortelloni of ricotta with butter and sage' in Italian?" Or "What is the Italian for *Hausgemachte lasagne mit Spinat?*" Or, come to think of it, for "*pitsa margarita, s prostym tomatnym sousom*"? Then one could proceed to pose a whole menu of still more toothsome linguistic conundrums, such as the Italian equivalent of the red or green *cazunzei* from the Dolomites, served with poppyseed butter, or the Italian term for *zuppa sarda*.

Mind you, the more this line of inquiry reminds you of Ionesco's play *The Lesson*, the less at home you will feel in the new London I'm now describing, apart from a handful of time-frozen institutions like Aspinalls whose continued existence, anyway, rather hangs by a thread. It almost seems that the surreal object of the whole nightmarish exercise is to imagine a group of Belgians in Harrods, shortly before its mercurial owner goes back to Egypt, arguing whether the French word *shopping* can be translated into the English language, or a group of Russians walking into the House of Lords, just days before it becomes an American theme park, and debating sullenly among themselves whether the Russian word *demokratiya* has some local equivalent.

It was another narrow escape for me, then, from the anguished pleasure of the Season, anguished because contrived, deracinated, and just short of perverse. And here I sit on the patio, carefully paved four centuries ago and cared for by anonymous, gnarled, brown hands ever since, thinking that the damson plums above my head are ripe and real, and have a name. In a couple of weeks' time I'll be making a journey by car to the Argentario on the Tuscan coast, and there again I will sit, on another terrace, thinking lazily that the giant watermelon shielded from the sun by the beach umbrella is neither a racial slur nor a class symbol, but simply a pitilessly quartered green sphere which the gods have invented for the amusement of thirsty children.

And then, come autumn, there will be Venice, where the world really ends. Not the way Italy ends here, at Santa Maria di Leuca, or as England does at Dover, with a precipitous drop into the sea, but the way a bodily injury heals itself or an evil spell is lifted, gradually, unobtrusively, yet irreversibly. No more restaurants serving foreign food, no more playing with cardsharps, no more German lasagne, Belgian shopping, and Russian democracy, no more conversations about nothing. No more leaving Venice.

A big red and yellow butterfly has just alighted on the keyboard of my portable. It must be an omen, a sign that I am right.

... the effect of all this on the Londoners' psyche

XVIII The Argentario

The Man from Uncle

Now that I think of it, I realize it was my own poor mother who told me that there is much too much food in my impressions of Italy. Listen my only begotten, she complained by telephone from New York, what with all your extravagant food descriptions, delightful food tropes, and revealing food analogies, you probably don't even have half a minute to wolf down a ham sandwich leaning over the kitchen sink. She does not understand Italy, my mother. Here the sociology of food *is* sociology, and the New York equivalent of instructing the cook or choosing the restaurant is meeting with your banker or broker. After all, just because all those Americans talk about money incessantly does not mean they don't make it hand over fist.

Consider Martin Frankel, the cybernetic master of disguise who seems to have disappeared from the face of the earth, to say nothing of Greenwich, Connecticut, with $2 billion. Does anyone suppose *he* used to talk about money like he didn't have any? Well, I'm the Martin Frankel of *astice alla catalana*, nay its Willi Münzenberg, its Kim Philby, and every half-decent cook within the fifty-mile radius of Port'Ercole has come to beware my dangerous attentions. That's just the way it is over here, in the hard, ruthless, man-eat-lobster world that is the Tuscan coast in summertime.

Even the Central Intelligence Agency, by far the world's dimmest bunch of ruffians, is beginning to catch on to the fact that eating is more than the traditional Italian form of thinking: increasingly, it is the fashionable European alternative to spying. Perhaps they are now even using James Jesus Angleton's recipe archive from the time he was stationed here – not that they'd give him any credit, mind you – and then P2, of course, must have supplied them with some useful little menus, especially of Sicilian dishes. Whatever the reason, spook activity around Harry's Bar in Venice, as well as around its Mark Birley namesake in London, is said to be at its highest in years, with types like Peter Jacobs and Thomas Corbally invariably getting the best tables. Chic restaurants, for the American spook community, are now what bookshops used to be for agents of the Comintern. Who can ever forget the Zeitgeist in Shanghai, where Richard Sorge used to buy his beach thrillers?

Anyway, Father Jacobs is described by the press here as "the strange priest tied to the fugitive financier Martin Frankel." A Jewish convert to Catholicism and now *un prete da jet-set* with a parish in Rome's Trastevere, Jacobs appears to have been in trouble before, with the Archdiocese of New York, for opening a swanky restaurant of his own called The Palantine. Tom Corbally, a partner in Kroll Associates, who introduced history's biggest thief to Jacobs in the first place – along with Tom Bolan, Robert Strauss, and a host of other political notables – is known in England as "the man who uncovered the Profumo affair." Having dined with Corbally a number of times, I can testify that he too knows a thing or two about linguine with clam sauce, and how to tuck in a well-starched napkin.

And speaking of dim, I simply cannot resist the following rosy reminiscence. Fifteen years ago, when I was courting a rich man's daughter, Kroll Associates was paid a commensurately large amount of money to find out everything there was to know about me. An inconspicuous larrikin in a beige trench-coat arrived to interview some people I knew, and before answering any of his questions they naturally asked him what the whole thing was about. "Mr. Navrozov is applying for a job," the spook ventured in his best tones of sweet dulcimer, "and we're doing a check of his personal background." Needless to say, no sooner was the three-letter word out of his mouth than every member of the assembled company fell over laughing: "Navrozov! Applying for a job! Come on, own up, you're a private dick! And a lousy one at that!" The moral of the story, I suppose, is that while American spooks will not become more bright by eating in fancy restaurants, they may, given enough time and $2 billion spending money, become a little more worldly.

But enough dark hints and playful imputations. Now begins the main strand of this troubled narrative, because Anna, our cook of the last three cloudless seasons here, has just got herself a regular job. This, you understand, is the kind of tragedy that can only happen in an Italian resort town, at the exact point of contact between the always undeserving rich, meaning the summer people, and the frequently idle poor, those who live here all year round. "Anna! How could she? After all we've done for her!" The reader can add what boilerplate cries of outraged virtue seem apposite. So, wiping off my man-eat-lobster smile and putting on the conspiratorial air of perfect nonchalance, I had to go out and investigate the surrounding countryside in search of a new cook. Even in flowered shorts tight around the belly, I'm sure I looked like the man from Kroll.

The first applicant, much recommended by the uncle of one friendly restaurant owner, displeased everybody by arriving at the house a good hour before the scheduled audition – yes, *prova* can thus be solemnly translated – and was without an apron. Even more alarmingly, she looked like a real witch. At first I tried to rationalize, of course, by recalling the perfectly charming sorceress from Verdi's *Un Ballo in Maschera* who gathered wild herbs by the light of the moon and very probably had an excellent way with light summer soups, but was finally dissuaded when I overheard Giovanna muttering to herself what sounded like magic spells while being shown around the kitchen. Also, the contralto in Verdi was always young, raven-haired, and buxom, whereas the real witch was not. In fact, she was extremely thin, and I'm not so deracinated as to forget that in my native tongue the word "thin" also means "evil."

Without so much as a fair trial, Giovanna was told a little white lie. Our friendly restaurateur informed her that the rich Russian gentleman had found somebody else for the job, whereupon, having taken the usual precautions and reassuring himself all the while with one or another of the great honeyed mantras of meliorism, the man from Kroll went out again among the shadows of Mediterranean night. This time the applicant was recommended, funnily enough, by the owner of a famous beach restaurant in Ansedonia called La Strega, which means The Witch. Graziella, who came only fifteen minutes late for her appointment and wore an apron, was a good deal more comely and not nearly as crazy as Giovanna, yet in some strange, intractable way she seemed to be the witch's younger, healthier, and slightly less jaundiced sister. She was none the less given her *prova*, and I must honestly say that on the opening night the aubergines in our plates had been fried so delicately that the audience wept tears of contrition.

But then, like a summer storm out of a clear blue sky, an unexpected telephone call put an end to that bout of love and repentance. It was the witch Giovanna, shouting obscenities into the receiver, to the effect that she knew just what we'd been up to, that she wouldn't let us get away with it, no, not for anything, that she'd given us the best years of her life, well, hours anyway, and petrol for the car, and now we're lying and saying we hired somebody else, when in fact we only found Graziella yesterday. I felt at once that all my conspiratorial techniques had failed me miserably, that I had been followed, observed, perhaps secretly taped. "But... how did you know?..." I stammered out the pathetic plaint of every exposed spy in history. "Because Graziella is my sister, that's how, you numbskull!" came the reply.

So Graziella had to be fired too, to avoid complications, and both had to be paid off in a rather generous way. Despite this act of largess, admittedly tainted by cowardice, a few days later a group of house guests returning from the beach found two enormous black cats barring the front gate of the villa. They said they had never seen anything quite like it, and I understand exactly what that dark portent means.

It means, among other things, that my mother is right to worry about what her sole begotten is eating.

… that all my conspiratorial techniques had failed me

XIX The Argentario

The Show of Shows

Say what you will, there is no dame like an Italian *grande dame*. Though based on my own experience, this claim is easily supported by any amount of independent observation as the number of subjects to whom it applies, given that the history of the aristocracy in this country resembles schematic representations of nuclear fission in old physics textbooks, is simply vast. Moreover, the rest of Italian women – those who do not fit the type under discussion for all sorts of reasons – none the less model themselves, and their defining affectations and aspirations, on the aspect of the female character which is not often illuminated by fashion magazines, television, or Hollywood. In that very real sense in which American women want to be thin, French women want to be clean, and English women want to be elegant, Italian women want most of all to be grand.

There was a *grande dame* who came to dinner the other day, and she was telling a story. I cannot remember exactly what her story was about, but she was talking about American art and went on to postulate, plausibly enough I should say, that artists like to bite the hand that feeds them, meaning their patrons. At which point I interrupted her, because, as happens now and then, a witticism had begun to form in the back of my mind, and then rolled over to the front of my head like a loose dumbbell, and then I simply couldn't keep it in any longer and out it tumbled: "The *invisible* hand, you mean." Those who sympathize with my predicament will appreciate my reasoning. The patrons are mostly wealthy, right? And wealth makes you think of Adam Smith, and Adam Smith makes you think of the invisible hand, and the idea of biting a hand which is invisible is pretty funny.

Which, clear as daylight, was the only reason I'd interrupted her, and yes, of course I agree, in the final analysis it's a stupid joke. But aren't all jokes stupid in the final analysis? And don't you think that a friendly chuckle, or at worst an admonitory pause, would be called for at that juncture, even if the interrupted party had something original and vital to tell about American art and artists? To say that the *grande dame* froze is like saying that God liked the world. No, she simply turned to stone, which was naturally the costliest kind of marble. I can only compare her with Osip Mandelshtam's "neoclassical shawl" cascading in bar-relief about Anna Akhmatova's shoulders unto all eternity. She was Phèdre, she was Niobe, she was the shadow of the evaporated mother in Hiroshima. I had interrupted her in her role of *grande dame*, and to say that I felt like a rotter is like saying there is some good food in this part of Tuscany.

Let me change tack for a moment, because I just came back from the darkest Maremma countryside which I had been scouring for *culatello*, a kind of ham which literally begins where other hams leave off, to bring back with me to Venice. Every bar, in just about every one-bar town in the mountains that I visited, had the following announcement in the window. I swear I am not hamming it up for effect:

DENJI SHOW

presents

A ONE-HOUR-LONG SPECTACLE.

International Attractions. Jugglers. A Charming Trained Doggy Number.
A Giant Squid, over 500 kg. of Gelatinous Muscle.
An Anaconda, Strangler of Men.

INCREDIBLE BUT TRUE! LIVE CROCODILES.
A young woman cheats death in a crystal bowl full of scorpions, black widows,
tarantulas, and poisonous snakes of every description.
And, for the first time ever, *LIVE PIRANHA!*

Here some cynical sourpuss may grumble that the great Denji Show of Orbetello is not so unlike what passes for entertainment in the drawing rooms of Belgravia, to say nothing of the bedrooms of Manhattan. That is not my point here, but the carper would be right in a sense. To be grand, in the sense defined by the history and traditions of Europe, is above all to entertain and be entertained in accordance with established convention, the very principle I had had the temerity to subvert with my dumb joke about the invisible hand. The dumb joke was that it was I who had bitten the hand of civilized custom. The dumb joke was on me.

All of which is to say that the ladies of Manciano, Magliano, and Pitigliano, who come down from the mountains to the noisy and shameless seaside, and attend the first performance of the Denji as if it were a season première at La Scala, are being grand in a way in which their British or American counterpart, who buys a DVD player instead, cannot even imagine herself wishing to be, to say nothing of being. Because here life is about being grand at whatever social level has fallen to your share. Elsewhere, life is about keeping up with the Joneses.

It is interesting to note in this connection that the Michelin Guide, fat, red, French, and yet the world's chief justiciar and uncorrupt arbiter of gastronomic achievement, awards stars to just two Venetian establishments apart from the implacable Harry's Bar ("Patrons are reminded," Cipriani writes on the menu, "that the ringing of cellular phones may interfere with the preparation of risotto"). These two are Da Fiore, in the fashionable San Polo quarter, and a place called Autoespresso, with the gloomy and slightly venal address of Via Fratelli Bandiera 34, deep in the industrial wilderness of Marghera suburbs.

Whether in Florence or in Venice, in Orbetello or in Marghera, come along and watch an Italian woman, even of the lowliest station, order her morning coffee at the local bar, ticket in divinely manicured hand. Properly considered, and mindful of the algebraic assumption that the *x* of coffee and the *y* of milk are the only conceivable variables in any equation describing what she is actually about to order, this really is entertainment to end all entertainment. This is both Maria from Manciano, trembling at the sight of *la gigantesca piovra di oltre 500 kg. di musculo gelatinoso*, and Violetta from *La Traviata* on the Milan stage, swooning Swinburneanly among orchids and lilies, in a single burst of blinding theatricality:

"I'll have mine with just a little foam, please, but not too much foam, and in a glass, and not too hot. No, not a *macchiato*, just an ordinary cappuccino with a little foam. Just a little bit. And in a glass. And not too hot."

"Can I have one with approximately half the usual amount of foam, but I would like the foam to be extremely hot, and the coffee not hot at all. Just warm, please. Yes, warm. No, the coffee warm, and the foam extremely hot. No, not a *macchiato* with very hot foam, just a cappuccino."

"Do me a favour, make me a cappuccino just the way you made it for the man there, but with less foam, more like a *macchiato*, but yes, with the chocolate, and I would like the coffee to be near room temperature. No, not a *macchiato* with somewhat tepid coffee, I would just like a normal cappuccino like the man over there was having."

"I'll have my usual *latte macchiato*. But today, could you make it just a little less strong, and with just a smudge of foam? No, actually I won't have that. I'll have a camomile tea, but not too much camomile, like you put yesterday. That was too strong for me. I *was* going to tell you, but then my sister called from Padua."

Now compare these glimpses of Italian womanhood with the scene I witnessed last spring at the Florian in Venice. Two American women approach the bar, and one of them says to the barman: "*Latte, per favore.*" He puts a magnificently appetizing glass of milk, all beady from condensation and reminiscent in its opacity of Bianca Sforza's pearls in the famous portrait, on the neatly folded and very starched napkin in front of her. "No," she says loudly, as if speaking to a deaf man, "*latte*, I wanted a *latte*." "But miss," he replies in English, "*latte* is milk, no?" "No," she says, "I mean, *latte*!" And then, hopelessly, turning to walk out of the most famous café in the world: "Aw, forget it."

…watch an Italian woman order her morning coffee at the local bar

XX Venice

The Values of Unreal Estate

I must write something about the man from Palm Beach who has come to stay, which is awkward for two reasons. One problem is that bashing the Ugly American is a cliché of European journalism, only slightly less ugly than the idea that Europe – the United States of Europe, ideally – ought to emulate the United States in every particular. Here I hasten to assure the reader that what follows is not an attempt at generalization: I'm sure Pat Buchanan, for instance, isn't in the least like my guest, nor were Emerson, Emily Dickinson, T. S. Eliot… Who else is there? The other problem is that I *am* about to vent my spleen, which, inevitably, will sound monstrously inhospitable. All I can say there, by way of apology, is that I have been pushed to the limit.

Let me start at the beginning. There was a time when the very landscape of the United States – Manhattan's skyscrapers, enormous cars with tail fins, writers drunk on Bourbon, aircraft carriers that ruled the waves – intimidated the European visitor, forcing him into a spasm of revaluation: what was he, for all his descent from some Norman swordsman, who was this tweedy, balding, hesitant insect in the path of the Chrysler Building? But the world moved on, Moscow began making its submarines of seamless titanium, Hong Kong built its share of skyscrapers. Obviously the stock prices of Internet companies are no substitute for a landscape, nor is Kosovo for Korea.

The tables have turned. Hugh Grant is a matinée idol. Intellectually and spiritually, it is Europe – its surviving beauty, its superior serenity, its continued existence – which is now deeply insulting to my American guest. And if I had recognized this beforehand as his Achilles' heel and set out to offend him deliberately, I could not have picked a better place than Venice, and our apartment over the Grand Canal, in the palazzo where Byron lived. Location, location, location.

The American is rich, you see. He owns a house on South County Road from whose windows you can see the Breakers. Tour buses pass by, touting celebrity: "There's Ivana's house over there!" Naturally, he has a keen sense of his place in the upper tier of the social pyramid. And here he is with his monogrammed luggage from T. Anthony in New York, delivered by motorboat into our palazzo's cathedral of an *androne* with a sculpted wellhead of white Istria stone for a reliquary. He has no idea who Byron is ("Byron who?" he asks, and I cannot answer him because I fear that he has never heard of anybody called Lord, nobody who is white I mean). He does not suspect that his matching set of luggage is manufactured in Vicenza. He has never learned to eat spaghetti without a knife. But he has eyes and by his own admission he knows a thing or two about real estate, and this is his downfall. Location, location, location.

He is insulted from the start, from his first glimpse of that other life, my life, a life I have every right to characterize, on the basis of income tax returns and sworn affidavits from intimate friends, as the life of a poor struggling writer. He does not say "But how can you afford this?" because it isn't me and my success or failure which are on his mind just then, but his own power, and his own exalted position in the social pyramid. Location, location, location. He takes the private lift up to the galleried hall of the *piano attico*. Just look at all this marble, he says to himself of the honey smoothness of the *pastellone* floors, brick dust clotted with linseed oil and polished over the centuries to the sheen of cloudy amber. "Marble?" Marble, marble. Ornately moulded ceilings. Oak parquet. All awash with autumnal light. Yes, Lord Byron slept here, and not always alone, while there, from that mullioned window overlooking the Grand Canal at San Tomà, he would lean out in his shirt sleeves, waving to the gondoliers below, but that is not the point. The point is, he knows a thing or two about real estate, and now his world view is tottering, and the ever-triumphant voice of the Lake Worth tour guide that has sustained his prestige, and injected his family with the sweet, heady sense of earthly achievement, is so much faint patter.

Tottering, but not crumbling. Not a single fissure, not even the smallest chink. I marvel at its earthquake-proof elasticity, which brings to mind the purges in Stalin's Russia, when a faithful old Bolshevik, with a lifetime of ardent service to socialism behind him, would open the door to his ostensible brethren of the NKVD who had come to arrest his ailing bedridden wife as a Bolivian spy and a trafficker in gold bullion. And guess what? More often than not, that poor sod's world view – rendered elastic by a thousand similar exercises in years past – managed to absorb the shock of the absurd, recover, and go on functioning until the last circle was squared in the back of his own head with the aid of several grams of lead.

The European, his intellectual shell crushed like that of an egg by the architecture of New York and the power of America, used to fall silent, more often than not for the rest of his natural life. The American, flattened like a ball of Wrigley's by the beauty of Venice and the luxury of Europe, talks even more than usual. He talks to waiters in restaurants. He shows wallet snaps of his children to shop girls selling masks. He talks to gondoliers by the Rialto, and the remarkable thing is that all the while he does not seem to know whether he, Haroon al Rashid in the disguise of Joe Blow, wants to be treated by these strangers as a prince or a pauper. This is a classic of infantile psychology, a mental manoeuvre, incidentally, beloved of Dostoevsky: if someone snubs him as an ordinary American tourist who thinks *involtini* are a kind of fish, he turns capricious ("But I *told* him I don't want any fish! *Or* veal!") and vindictive ("Right, there goes *his* tip!"), but if you indulge him, he becomes suspicious ("They're trying to rip me off!") and defensive ("What does *she* want? I bet you anything she knows *exactly* who I am!").

He is what they call a piece of work. With me he thinks he can be "open," meaning talk frankly, and all he wants to talk about frankly is money: why I make so little of it, why I spend so much of it, why he makes so much of it, why he spends so much of it, why he doesn't make more of it, why I should make more of it, how I should make more of it, how everybody should make more of it… Mark Twain, in one of his European travelogues, makes up a conversation between two peasants, Swiss I think, who discuss cow dung *ad infinitum*, and until now I used to think this was just a flight of fancy, a light-hearted, inconsequential squib. No, it turns out that it is perfectly possible to watch, breathe, and adore money twenty-four hours a day, as if banknotes were an agricultural fertilizer and man were a stalk of seakale beet in an inaccessible Alpine village.

I now understand that, for him, reality – American reality first and foremost, of course, and colonial reality to the extent it can be translated into imperial terms, real-estate and other – is form, while money (which translates itself according to the current rate of exchange, including commission) is content. The content fills the form the way a coloured liquid may be observed to follow the contours of a glass vessel, or the way bronze is cast. But such an image is much too concrete and tangible, too phenomenal I would say, to do any real justice to his world view. Money, for him, operates on a submolecular level. It is atomic. The nape of a woman's neck, the feather of a seabird, the oar of a boat, all of this real estate is run through the spectrograph of his mind and analysed for carbon content. And this palazzo in Venice is so rich in fossil carbon!

When after three days he finally leaves on the first morning flight to Paris, I feel I have aged beyond words. That evening I meet for the first time the Roman coloratura Cecilia Bartoli, in Venice to sing Vivaldi, whom a mutual friend brings to the house:

> Dite, oimè, ditelo al fine:
> Deggio vivere o morir?
> Sta mia vita in sul confine,
> Pronta è già l'alma ad uscir!

She is a great beauty, dark, with huge, dramatic eyes like moist horse chestnuts and the proverbial alabaster skin, and as I listen to the woman lamenting in the Venetian idiom of Scipione Maffei that her life is on the brink and her soul about to depart, I cannot stop looking at her neck and her shoulders, in silhouette against the carved balusters of the upper gallery where my son is hiding with a bouquet of wild flowers.

Looking, and thinking: what does that cost? And who can afford it?

… the Roman coloratura Cecilia Bartoli, in Venice to sing Vivaldi

XXI Venice

Not the Venice of the North

I have always disbelieved those who would argue that the topography of a country, that is to say its purely geophysical characteristics, is dominant in the shaping of the personality of its people. Stalin used to call them vulgarizers of Marxism, and shoot them, but we in the West may simply murmur that they exaggerate and are often wrong. One need only to spend a few weeks in Sardinia, where the native island culture effectively insulates the inhabitants from the sea, to understand that so much of historiography is like Freudian psychology, in that it is two-thirds *ex post facto* reasoning and one-third old wives' tales.

Last week I conducted a fairly inexpensive experiment to test the materialist thesis against which I had been prejudiced anyway by spending a weekend in Amsterdam, a place where I had never been before. Amsterdam is called the Venice of the North. Why Venice? Well, don't you see, it has all those canals, just like Venice, and the boats and the bridges. My thinking was that as the airline tickets were cheap, the hotels in the doldrums of low season, I do not use cannabis, and was bringing my wife as chaperone, the worst that could happen was that the thesis would be disproved – Amsterdam would turn out to be *not* the Venice of the North – and I would return home with the satisfaction of having been right all along. Which is exactly what happened, and probably I would have let the matter rest without bothering to gloat about it had the collapse of the thesis not been so spectacular and, in some strange ways, so unexpected.

The first thing of which I am aware when sober is the sound of speech, and the first place that Amsterdam brought to mind was Copenhagen. This is because like the Danes, and Scandinavians generally, the Dutch speak a kind of deracinated Hyperamerican with a facility that is at once arresting and repugnant. When one listens to the answer to the simplest question, say about the way to one's hotel, one is conscious of observing something unnatural, yet titillating, like some cabaret exhibition of dexterity imagined by Magritte involving a snake, a bird cage, and three small oranges. Then, if the questions and the corresponding answers become more complex, the circus act image recedes and is supplanted in one's mind by similes from magazine articles on artificial intelligence and stills from Hollywood films about aliens in human guise:

"Do you speak English? I phoned for a taxi an hour ago, and it's still not here."

"Theresalottafraffic authere yaknow. Yah yah okay I givemacall."

It helps not at all that visually Dutch is so close to English, so that the visitor's eye, bewildered by shop signs, keeps sending confused messages of alarm to the brain, roughly along these lines: "Citizen, you have been asleep for 311 years. It is now the year 309 EU, and we are all speaking Prosperanto. The English word 'house' is 'huis' in Prosperanto. The word 'bread' has become 'banana brood with nuts.' The word 'ecu' has been changed to 'eurouble.'"

…I can still cross the Rialto and eat local soft-shell crabs

The other place I thought Amsterdam was like is Chicago, because the Dutch automaton's deracinated speech from the future is very much like the apparently deracinated culture – including dress, manners, conversation, and cuisine – of most large American cities, which are unfailingly comical in their provincial insecurity. No doubt this insecurity is fuelled from New York, and exacerbated weekly by the culture supplements of the *New York Times*, so that no restaurant chef in Chicago can put a T-bone steak on the menu without something like *au romarin et anchois truffés* after it unless he wants to get himself arrested as a White Supremacist, any more than a theatre director in Detroit can put on a thoughtful production of *Pinocchio* without being accused of anti-Semitism. Anyway, looking for a Dutch dish in Amsterdam is like looking for hash brownies in Riyadh, or asking CBS to screen an art film entitled *The Protocols of the Elders of Zion* in prime time.

"Do you speak English? I'm trying to find somewhere that serves Dutch food."

"Sure, there's a fantastic Cantonese place on the Reguliersdwarsstraat."

Why yes, one almost finds oneself thinking at that point, the Cantonese on the Reguliersdwarsstraat, of course, how could I've been so foolish. It's like forgetting about the Pakistani on the Oosterdokskade!

"Good Dutch food?"

"Duck, they've got good duck. Great service, nice, really nice place."

This brings me to an aspect of character of the Venetians of the North which an impartial observer would describe as a certain denseness, whereas a hostile, irresponsible, prejudiced person might let fly with the altogether slanderous charge of unadulterated stupidity. In this, Amsterdam reminds me of Cambridge and that tract of midge-swarming, disease-ridden, blithely flowering swampland called East Anglia to which Holland is, I have to admit, geophysically related far more closely than it is to Venice. A friend of mine once took a tailcoat, with its regulation stains of claret and vomit, to the dry cleaners in Cambridge. The elderly woman in charge inspected it, stroked the stains tenderly, and announced: "I' very nice, that, bu' I wun't know wha' to charge you, luv, 'cuz here on the back i's long like a coa', bu' 'ere on the front i's short like a jackit." Surely you've had one of these in before, he remonstrated, with all the May Balls at Cambridge over the last hundred years? "We 'ave, an' I ne'er know wha' to charge 'em!" answered the woman with a flirtatious chuckle.

Naturally enough, from the point of view of architecture the spire-capped, haematite-redbrick town is reminiscent of Manhattan's surviving shreds of New Amsterdam, somehow reordered within the space of Boston. But although perfectly explicable historically, this impression only serves to enhance the eerie sense of alienation from language, time, and place which grabs hold of the visitor on arrival. Like a fool I trudged to the Rijksmuseum, in the hope that the fire of art would soon cauterize the infectious feeling – readers who wish me to carry on in this florid vein may send a cheque for £1 with large SAE enclosed – that the town was taking the mickey. I will not say anything about the Vermeers, because the Vermeers are in fact quite deft and very likely worth the candle, but the "Night Watch Room"! I thought they had slipped something into my duck at the Cantonese joint, and that I was hallucinating.

For the first time I understood the homespun fraud that is "history of art," as taught at universities, in all its threadbare ubiquity. The enormous hall of the Rijksmuseum gives the famous picture pride of place, but it is surrounded on all sides by dozens of paintings by Rembrandt's contemporaries. This is meant to show how much better – greater, I think, is the preferred art history term – he was than anybody else painting in the early 1600s, though what it actually shows beyond reasonable doubt is that he was exactly like them, and I mean exactly, down to the last shiny buckle on the last of the idiotic black cones those people used as hats. The pervasive, ponderous conformity of both the painters and their red-nosed, white-jaboted, black-breeched subjects, squeezed together in large bunches one on top of the other, like office workers packing the lift at lunchtime, makes for an unforgettably hideous spectacle, something like a Russian newspaper cartoon from the Japanese War of 1905 or an illustration from some mimeographed brochure about the Yellow Menace.

Which brings me back to the Cantonese on the Reguiliersdwhatever, and to the reasonable suggestion that the countries of Europe, already reduced to the status of imperial cantons, are not far from achieving the degree of deracinated uniformity allotted them in that epochal collusion of Moscow and Washington known as Brussels. Canals and bridges will not save their souls as they have until now saved the soul of Venice, whose survival had been preconditioned by the lingering disunity of Italy and made possible by the recalcitrant archaism of the region's myriad discordant social institutions. The grandees painted by Rembrandt all wore cone-shaped hats, but when the time came, they all donned baseball caps; they all said grace before supper, but when the time came, they all lit up giant spliffs; they all loved their neighbour, but when the time came, they all got together and sold their country down the river.

The grandees of Italy's regions, who all ate different food, said grace in different languages, and loathed their neighbours, were never in a position to perform such a hat trick. As a result of this whim of history, for which the topography of Venice is perhaps no more than a useful foil and a beautiful symbol, I can still cross the Rialto to the Madonna and eat local soft-shell crabs, which are now in season in the lagoon. For diversity is not listening to rap music in Vienna, or speaking Urdu with a taxi driver in Paris, but living in Venice like a Venetian. Which is precisely what I, chastened by my experience of Amsterdam, propose to do until the Grand Canal becomes a municipal parking facility and Brussels orders the Frari to warehouse frozen bananas.

I am no flibbertigibbet. I would happily live in Chicago as a Chicagoan. But how can one?

XXII Venice

Living Souls

Last spring I promised myself that I would write in greater detail about Baron F— , who liberated me from Florentine bondage by letting me the *attico* at Corte Tron, with its lifesaving terrace looking over the courtyard of the Palazzo Volpi and beyond, to the motionless cranes over the ruined Fenice. Almost a year has passed, and we are still fast friends; last week I improvised a dish, along the general lines of Louisiana gumbo, with some mallards he had shot on a remote islet in the lagoon; moreover, Michael Palin has now exposed him as a public figure in a television series about Hemingway. In short, in print as in life, I can call him by his Christian name.

It is quite the first time, incidentally, that this business of calling a person by his given name has any significance in my life, and I want to put that new sensibility in a broader context. The other night I was talking to a young woman about a dinner party in Porto Ercole we had both attended in the summer, where she and her friend the hostess were the only Italians. The other guests, with a whole pashmina of marriageable girls among them, belonged to the broad, fast, first world that is New York, Paris, and the new London. Ordinarily, in my former social hypostasis, I would have remembered with perfect clarity who they all were, especially the girls, by name and surname, stated occupation, last known address and mobile phone number, as well as whose jokes they laughed at, what shoes they wore, whom they were likely to marry in the end, and whether it would be worth the trouble to get invited to the weddings. This time, nothing. A sociopath's blank.

I realized just how much I had been spoiled by Venice in the intervening period, by Venice where the person with whom one is speaking is by definition a public figure, a permanent feature of the civic landscape, who has been here, perhaps in the form of his ancestors yet in this very armchair opposite, for two hundred, eight hundred, twelve hundred years. One's awareness of one's interlocutor, in such circumstances, matures gradually, progressing in small increments from the superficial and ritualized to the covert and coveted, and the privilege of addressing a person by his Christian name comes with the social territory that is painstakingly, but above all slowly, explored. This habit of social slowness, which is really a kind of wary sloth, is in vivid contrast with the manners of the first world and even of the second, which in Italy would include Milan and to some extent the new Berlusconi-Murdoch, television-executive, wheel-of-fortune Rome.

There, in those newer, more intoxicating, less maigre worlds, the very firmament is in ferment, with human particles borne by diverse currents appearing and disappearing from view like snowflakes in a storm, with the effect that your interlocutor at a dinner party – all the more so if she is a pretty girl looking over your shoulder in no fewer than three directions at once – must be apprehended, appraised, fixed, and charmed all of an instant, whereupon the trauma of transience, dislocation, and accident is momentarily allayed and social life reacquires a semblance of meaning.

Quickness, rapidity, rapacity are the jabs of the anaesthetic that makes it all possible there, just as reticence, or perhaps dignity, is what you have to inject yourself with in Venice "if you want to have a good time."

It is interesting that the bit of hackwork aired on the BBC made the same point, albeit in a somewhat more politically tremulous key. The presenter noted Alberto's manifest "lack of urgency," and even murmured that "the word languid could have been coined" for him. "I ask what I should call him," Palin went on, "should it be Signor Franchetti, or perhaps Alberto? He purses his lips gently, as if acknowledging some distant, unspecific pain.

"'Perhaps *Barone?*' he suggests."

Alberto may not be Venice, but he is as close to it as you can get without building a bridge of fine Istria stone between your pancreas and your liver. He is something more than a good old boy, he is an archetype, one of a tiny handful of eminent Venetians who are to their nation what Gogol's "old world landowners" were to the Russia of his day. The author of *Dead Souls* never finished his "poem," which he had envisioned as a variation on Dante – only the part corresponding to the *Inferno* survives, and half of the *Purgatorio* – and thus the modern chronicler of Venice can plunge directly into the sort of book that might have been Gogol's *Paradiso*, without at any time feeling that he is treading on hallowed ground. And, insofar as what he aims to capture are the living souls of Venice, he must begin with Alberto.

As our landlord and neighbour, Alberto used to arrive on the terrace with a mess of dinner invitations for us in his pockets, and naturally we always wanted to accept all of them. A truly social foreigner in London would consider himself an outcast, perhaps a prisoner, if all of a sudden he had to limit herself to three hundred dinner parties a year. Alberto would clear his throat, adjust a loose vine, fiddle with the ashtray. "No, but you know, you are going too fast. You cannot be so fast in Venice. You will burn out. You must be very careful. Why not have drinks with the M— on Tuesday, and then perhaps we can dine with G— on Friday, which will be very nice for you because they have a pleasant garden. But tomorrow I would like to suggest that you stay at home, and do nothing. No... thing at all. You will see, it would be much better."

"Can we go somewhere with your boat?"

"I do not think we should this week, no. No, we had better not. There is a terrible virus going round, you see. It is in the newspaper. I know many people who have it already."

Palin approached him to be the guide to Hemingway's haunts in Venice despite the fact that when the American writer came here, and was befriended by the Franchetti family, Alberto was ten. But what I find so remarkable is how the BBC's Virgil, or rather my Beatrice, gradually upstages the subject of that meandering documentary: The Man of Action, The Devil-May-Care Lover, The Celebrated Author and Worst Shot-Up Man in US seems to shrivel up and recede into the background of modern history as The Languid Nobleman, The Man in the Moth-Holed Khaki Sweater, The Proprietor of the Palazzo Tron who Never Replaces the Blown Lightbulb in the Hall and Drives a Boat the Size of a Child's Shoe emerges as a far more interesting and genuinely literary personage.

The famous boat (commercial value: none, not even with a fresh coat of paint, value of the engine, if the thing ever starts: $50) sank the other night, in mysterious circumstances. Alberto telephoned with the horrible news. Apparently he had left it on the Grand Canal, tied to one of the posts outside his door.

"What happened?"

"I cannot think. Certainly I had not moored her too fast, so it was not the tide that did it." His voice is ashen. "I think perhaps the fire brigade passed and sideswiped her."

"So what are you going to do now?"

"I went into the canal with a rope at low tide last night, to look for what was there."

"How? In your trousers?" I obviously don't know what else to say. Trousers? It was five degrees centigrade on the Sunday of the Madonna della Salute, and a driving wind from the north called *bora* was thrusting wet snow over Venice and the lagoon.

"No, I had removed my trousers. I managed to pull up the motor, and you know, it started on the first try. But the boat, no. I am afraid that is now completely lost. When the motor started at five o'clock this morning, I just smoked a cigarette and went to bed."

I suggest that the protagonist of this scene, the same man who would advise us to stay indoors last spring for fear of viral infection and nervous exhaustion, has been using a drug all his life – the tranquillizer called human dignity – to keep the world at bay. This is evident from his comportment in the face of loss, something with which all the great families of Venice are familiar. Alberto's have long lost the Palazzo Cavalli-Franchetti, built in the mid-1400s and occupied first by the Condottiere Cavalli, then by the Counts Pepoli, who established there the famous music academy of the *Rinovati*, then by Archduke Frederick of Austria, and finally by Alberto's great-grandfather, the noted composer Alberto Franchetti. And they have lost their other, even more splendid seat, the Ca' d'Oro, "perhaps the most famous house of the Grand Canal," according to the Eleodori *Palaces and Families*, "to be compared only to the Palazzo Ducale for the richness of its decorations," which was eventually bequeathed to Venice together with its important collection of paintings.

And now the boat. Now I ask you, is there anything in Hemingway's life and work that even comes close to this as a test of character?

… about Baron F—, who liberated me from Florentine bondage

XXIII Venice

The Lagoon and the Abyss

> What Exile from himself can flee?
>   To Zones, though more and more remote,
> Still, still pursues, where-e'er I be,
>   The blight of life – the demon, Thought.

Thus a previous occupant of our palazzo, Lord Byron. Romantic rubbish, you say? Venice not remote enough for him? Should have tried some other zone, freezing rain in October and forty below in March, shovel in hand and memories of a cigarette as one's principal divertissement? In the vulgar idiom of a less fortunate generation,

> Next morning the fog was all gone,
>   The furious waves calmed down,
> Before us arose Magadan,
>   The Kolyma zone's main town.

As I write this, with the gentle voice of Italian winter for a soundtrack, whimpering pitifully somewhere beyond the Arsenale just as the twentieth century has always been meant to whimper in farewell, there is but a single thought in my head, namely, that the Christian world as we know it is going to relive the history of totalitarian Russia in our lifetime. I look at the demon thought this way, and that; I turn it over in my mind, and look at it sideways, and then again in the face; I look at it in unaccountably frequent moments of happiness and during bouts of depression; dead drunk and stone sober; alone and in conversation with friends; but no matter how I look at it, I see no escape from what appears to be unavoidable. Not historically inevitable, mind you, because I am not fool enough to get worked up over theories of history, or entangle myself in ontological disputation; not divinely predestined, for roughly the same reason; but simply unavoidable, in the sense that an egg will surely crack if the huge leathery bottom of an adult hippopotamus comes to rest upon it.

I am not talking politics, either. Even if I come to believe, against all evidence to the contrary, that the ruling junta in Russia will suddenly terminate its continuing nuclear, chemical, and biological armament while the West curtails its own strategic disarmament, with the result that the United States, France, and Britain retain some viable deterrent against global blackmail in the years to come; or that a nameless American idealist, despite having neither campaign funds nor a political machine nor a fair press, will be elected president by a landslide, neither to invoke Averell Harriman in his inaugural address nor to lunch with Henry Kissinger the day after; or that the tomatoes offered for sale in a supermarket in Birmingham will become as real as the homegrown produce of Sant' Erasmo which I can still find on some mornings at the Rialto; even if I come to believe all that, and in the tooth fairy besides, I will conclude that the bad news balances the good 1:1 in the sense defined by the seller of sausages with a filling of horsemeat and partridge in an old Russian story, meaning one horse to one partridge.

Over Christmas I bought the "*Numero Millennium*" of the Italian current affairs weekly *Panorama*, mainly because the magazine's cover story, entitled "Welcome to the Twenty-First Century," was largely taken up with European Union statistics. Obviously, nobody with a desk job in Italy was going to work over the holidays, not even in Milan, and the issue had been printed well in advance, some desperate journalists having hit upon the ploy of publishing raw data in feverish anticipation of skiing in Cortina d'Ampezzo. Since I was probably that issue's only reader – everybody else was out buying giblets and stocking up on lentils – I must report the stale news it contained, in the form of the Index of Preparedness for the Future and another called the Index of Social Harmony. "Which of the fifteen member states of the European Union," the statisticians were asked, "is the most innovative and dynamic (*più dinamici e innovativi*)?" Last on the list was Italy. "Which European country affords the best opportunity of living in peace (*dove si vive più serenamente*)?" First on the list is Italy.

What I am saying here, politics apart, is that *Panorama*'s cockamamie sociologists are obviously right on the money. Like Lord Byron, the world is unhappy. It yearns to be innovative and dynamic. It wants new, stranger and stronger, sensations and experiences, not peace and homegrown tomatoes from Sant' Erasmo. It is only nominally Christian – as, anyway, was Byron – in the sense that it no longer feels Christ's wounds as its own, and certainly has no intimate, keenly remembered knowledge of any more recent wounds, and of any more efficient methods of inflicting them, than the Crucifixion. For the people of the United States and Europe – in whose hands the prosperity and the liberty of the world are still held provisionally – the zones less remote from physical suffering are something akin to the famous Steinberg cartoon of Manhattan, where Rhodes, Kerensky, Attlee, Hitler, Stalin, Attila, McCarthy, Napoleon, Mao, Nixon, Lincoln, Washington, Churchill, Franco, Henry VIII, Charles IX, Nicholas I, Gorbachev, Medici, and Milosevič make up a giant Pol Pot of schoolbook history twaddle whose relevance to the individual citizen of the West, *mutatis mutandis*, is infinitely smaller than the appeal of a nationally advertised brand of sportswear.

Which one of us, on being approached by a homosexual prostitute in the men's lavatory at Grand Central Station, most plausibly a Hollywood scriptwriter who was last paid for a story fifteen years ago and has since become a heroin addict, will give him $100 and whisper: "No, his life is not over. He can start again, maybe learning to weave baskets for a gallery in the Village, or to make funny-shaped pies for children's parties. Better yet, he can set up an Internet site, where even Siberian villagers can share his sad experiences and learn from them. He can change, get married, read Kant's *Prolegomena* on Saturday nights and the Bible on Sundays. At the very least he can become a real-estate broker. Did Saul not become Paul?" What I am saying here, I repeat, is that the world's accelerating slide into the totalitarian abyss is as culturally preconditioned as the likely self-destruction of the man in the lavatory. Politics, in view of the wholesale evisceration of democratic politics in America and Britain – to say nothing of the Russian and East European simulacrum that was never intended to supersede or impede the ruling Andropovite junta – are only a small factor in this process of degradation, and even the soundest possible electoral outcomes can no more reverse the trend than the unexpected, and frankly unlikely, gift of a hundred-dollar bill can change the life, and avert the death, of a degenerate moron on the skids.

The difference, heartbreaking as I feel it, is that the Christian world of today – still full of beauty, still God-abiding of a severe winter day, still verdant in springtime – is more like the doomed Lord Byron than it is like the HIV-positive scriptwriter. It is external circumstances that have changed. If a British peer of the realm in 1820, was, like Britain and the rest of the Christian world at the time, the undisputed master of his own destiny, even the wealthiest American of 180 years later is, like the United States of today, but one vector in a myriad other strategic quantities of which tomorrow is composed. It made no difference to Byron's future that the richest countries of his day were three times richer than the poorest, including the part of the world now called Pakistan. Today, it ought to make one hell of a difference to a Briton that the world's poorest countries are 77 times poorer than the richest, and that Pakistan has successfully tested medium-range nuclear weapons.

I don't know. I'm going to have some giblets with lentils for supper, smoke a Tuscan cigar, and see if that makes the perspective any more rosy.

... the gentle voice of Italian winter for a soundtrack

XXIV Venice

Acqua Alta

Last year, when I first came to live here – as bearer of the *Carta Venezia*, the photo-ID which entitles the city resident to buy water bus tickets at seventy-five cents instead of the tourist's $3, I have the right to say "live" rather than "visit" – I made a private pact with Neptune and the spirits of the lagoon. That's how we Russians are, just give us a nice little pact and some secret protocols, and you can keep your money, your girls, and your red Ferrari.

Leaving out some of the duller codicils, I can disclose that my principal obligation under the terms of the pact was never to throw a cigarette butt into the water. I never smoke less than a pack a day, and was perfectly used to flicking the yellow-filtered butts with a James Dean sort of moodiness onto the pavements of many a world capital, but here a manifest change comes over the most repulsive of God's creatures. Even the most recalcitrant provincial egotist in the myriapod mass of sightseeing brutes, who, when in Rome, would not think twice before scattering Hershey's wrappers on the floor of the Pantheon, may well hesitate before throwing his stupid rubbish into the hyaline stillness of a Venetian canal.

The vow was made to the Adriatic and the lagoon, rather than to the city, because I always knew that one day I would have to get myself a boat of my own, which is what I've recently done. However easy and peaceful it is to putter at three miles an hour through the canals of Venice, once you are out in the lagoon, where changing currents, submerged sandbanks, and treacherous fog are considered a serious challenge to experienced islanders, you are in the power of Neptune, who will at least soak you to the marrow of your bones by way of admonition, if not actually skewer you with his trident like a piece of vinegar-dressed *musetto* that, of a misty cold morning, goes so well with a glass of Treviso Cabernet. Neptune must be appeased, I reasoned, and at the risk of looking perfectly ridiculous I took to stuffing cigarette butts into my coat pockets, to throw them away later. I used to dump them in little heaps, like carnival confetti, right on the ground, on the indifferent, impersonal, unfeeling ground.

Now to alter course for a moment. I had dinner the other night with Edward Goldsmith, founder of *The Ecologist* magazine and brother of the late Sir James Goldsmith, the man who died while trying to save British sovereignty from the encroachment of a Europe where, to paraphrase an old prophesy in a way that is relevant to my personal concerns, the writers would be Dutch, the tax inspectors Albanian, and the vintners Finnish. We talked about wine, as it happens, which very few growers nowadays do not muck up with pesticides and stabilizers, about Alain de Benoist, about free-range chickens and organically raised vegetables, about liberty, about Monsanto, about Margaret Thatcher. But the spectral question, one whose invisible, clammy, embarrassing presence I felt all through dinner, was this: Are we spoiled? Are we just a couple of spoiled brats, sitting on this dining-room banquette at Aspinalls and bitching, like Marie-Antoinette with Maria Theresa, about

... one sunny day there came *acqua alta*

the world outside and whether gingerbread cake ought to be banned because it ruins digestion?

I do not think so. I think there exists an objectively demonstrable connection between human happiness and the integrity of life. This last, like the political sovereignty which Sir James fought to defend, is a quality, such as that of a chain possessed of certain tensile strength, rather than a quantity, measurable in chicken-in-the-pot and DVD-in-the-bedroom units. It is, furthermore, a connection that can be shown to exist at all economic levels, from – I nearly wrote "the humble gondolier" before realizing that this would rather impair my reputation as an astute social observer – from myself, the only genuinely poor man of my acquaintance, to my millionaire interlocutor Teddy Goldsmith.

You cannot be a bit of a fallen woman, or something of a virgin. Once the chain is broken, it doesn't matter what bribes the electorate has received in the process, and how many chickens there are now in every pot. For theirs are not chickens but reusable plastic effigies; theirs is not liberty but an ever-thinning mess of latitudes; theirs is not life but a general-issue simulacrum. I am not an environmentalist, or I would make the point by describing the degradation of the chain link by link, from plankton to fisherman to poet. Nor am I a political scientist, who could make the point by mapping the erosion of the rights of the individual in the present epoch of transnational government and multinational corporate interests. I am just a twenty-a-day smoker who vowed to Neptune he would not litter in the lagoon, and I'm making the integralist point as best I can.

One sunny day there came *acqua alta*, for the first time that year and my very first in Venice. It is easy to describe what this is like to another Russian, because it's exactly like the first snowfall, when the known landscape of yesterday is converted overnight into the surgical cotton warehouse of a Martian field hospital, while the banal, leafless tree branch outside your window that has been looking almost utilitarian since September suddenly takes on the irrational contours of a beautiful and profligate thought. The children are out in the street, horsing around in the newsworthiness of it all, knee-deep, as if, literally, there was no tomorrow, while the parents are uncharacteristically indulgent, as if their own childhood, along with everything that's ever gone right in their lives, has been restored to them in that blessed instant.

To a person who knows nothing and wants to know nothing of the transport of the elements – to somebody who would insist that a more urbane and forthright description be supplied him – I can say that *acqua alta* works exactly like the bathtubs of Claridge's, that great flagship of pre-war, afternoon-tea-perfect hydropneumatic engineering in London, whose porcelain vastness the water fills through the plugholes from below, rather than the taps from above, with the expensive consequence that, after the initial gurgle of welcome, it is utterly noiseless. Here in Venice the streets, which are rarely wider than a Claridge's bathtub, fill up through small plughole-shaped grates cut into paving stone with just the same plush noiselessness and the same efficient quickness born of the eagerness to please, to provide old-world value for money, to compete with the Hilton and win. The water rises, changing the aspect of the city and providing the resident with the excuse to buy special rubber boots that anyone but a sexual deviant would agree look like mediaeval armour, stays a few hours, and eventually recedes, leaving the cobblestones clean as a shop window and the occasional ground-floor shopkeeper cursing the day he turned down the offer to move to Mestre.

And my cigarette butts? They got washed away and ended up somewhere out in the lagoon, in an unwitting yet direct violation of my pact with Neptune. The ground of Venice and the islands, it turned out, is not as indifferent and impersonal as I and all the other transient *foresti* might have supposed, but is the solid shell of the liquid sea and part of its mystery. So too with the chain of well-being, whose healthiest sections – the ones least likely to snap right in front of me, the ones most certain to last me until absolute disillusionment settles in – I devote myself to seeking out and counting and recording. Only rarely does the chain show itself to be stronger than one has assumed, and as ever it is only nature that is capable of pleasant surprises and of teaching the cynical pupil a cynical lesson.

XXV Venice

The Leporello Aspect

A couple of months ago I was in Milan for an "Homage to Giorgio Strehler" at the Teatro alla Scala. This was Mozart's *Don Giovanni*, conducted by Riccardo Muti and with a cast that, at least to my unspoiled ears, represented the sort of perfection that one only reads about, ruefully, in yellowed reviews of the opera seasons one's parents attended. During the intermission, as I leafed through the souvenir programme, I realized I had a modest contribution to make to the literary study of Da Ponte's libretto, and that is the observation that while the *cavaliere* speaks plainly, Leporello, his *servo*, slips into the more fanciful conditional or subjunctive mood every time he feels he has a captive audience. The overall effect is that of hilariously coquettish temporizing. At the start of the second act, as the nobleman loses patience with his servant, he turns choleric and shouts the buffoon down: "*Non soffro opposizioni!*"

Now back to Venice, where I had to sign the lease on the apartment I am renting. The owner is a young girl in her twenties, recently orphaned. ("No father, no mother," says Walter Matthau in Elaine May's *A New Leaf*, "no sisters, no brothers. She's perfect.") In everything that concerns the management of her vast estate she relies on the lawyer who used to be a close friend of her mother's, Avvocato I—, and it was to his office in S. Croce that I had been asked to come at ten o'clock that morning. The lease had long been agreed, drawn up, faxed back and forth between the contracting parties, and although all sorts of fast ones had been pulled in the process, I had decided not to quibble and just get the thing over with. I was there to sign.

The subjunctive mood of verbs, used to express condition, hypothesis, contingency, or possibility, is rather underdeveloped in Russian grammar, but it exists in English as much as it does in Italian. Potentially, at least, because it is only when one finds oneself face to face with an Italian lawyer, intent on wasting his time at the expense of his client, a wealthy orphan, that one finally grasps the concept of language as a social instrument in all its ruthlessly grasping actuality. From ten to eleven-thirty the Avvocato spoke to me in interminable sentences where no verb had a suffix I had ever heard before and exotic particles whizzed by me like ricocheting bullets, which was mighty strange, I kept saying to myself, since the document had already been signed by his client. So what earthly reason could there be for all those conditions, hypotheses, contingencies, and possibilities?

I managed to sign the thing just before noon, but the Avvocato would not let me go. Still in his jolliest subjunctive, he launched into a discussion of Italian inefficiency – "in government! AND in finance!! and in *LAW!!!*" – which ended a full hour later with a perfectly simple statement, delivered by a pretty secretary using the indicative mood of the relevant verb, to the effect that he had a luncheon engagement in fifteen minutes. We shook hands and at quarter past one I finally crept away, thinking how marvellous it was that I wasn't the dumb sucker paying the bill. One hundred and ninety-five minutes to sign a piece of paper! If it hadn't been for that luncheon

... the only thing that's wrong with this country

entr'acte, I'm sure I would have had to hear a sermon on the general imperfection of man, perhaps in both the Venetian and the Milanese versions, and if he ever got tired of the subjunctive he might have treated me to a recital of the No. 82 vaporetto timetable between Piazzale Roma and Ponte dell' Accademia. No, no, I know, this is the whole point. That simply isn't done.

Having had some experience of litigation and lawyers in both the United States and Britain, I can declare that by those standards the behaviour of Avvocato I—, not by any means a fly-by-night operator or ambulance-chaser but a long-trusted family practitioner and pillar of the community, is shocking and absurd. Yet there are no lawyer jokes in Italy. Italians prefer to tell jokes about politicians and policemen, and I have an amusing little statistic that may help to explain why. According to *Corriere della Sera*, the total number of *Tangentopoli* indictments, that is, indictments ordered by prosecutors in the eight-year history of the "Clean Hands" corruption investigations in Italy, stands at 3146. The number of indictments actually granted by the courts is 1233. The number of actual convictions is 582. The number of people actually serving prison sentences is 4.

But the real reason why there are no lawyer jokes in Italy is that lawyers – like doctors, pharmacists, architects, engineers, accountants, surveyors – are professionals, and hence invulnerably, unshakably, immovably genteel. Can anyone think of a single American joke at the expense of an architect? Of an English joke about an engineer? Neither obvious upstarts like the politicians nor poor deadbeats like the *carabinieri*, Italian professionals are all of them pillars of the community and models of responsible citizenship. They are more than bourgeois professionals, they are professional bourgeois. They may not be revered, or even deeply respected, but making jokes about them is too much like cutting off your nose to spite your face. Thus a lawyer may be cheating an orphan, a surveyor may be soliciting a bribe, an accountant may be arranging the payoff for a contract killing, but they are each other's and everybody else's own, they are the community's flesh and blood, they are what everyone wants to be and is. Except for the class distinction that is their affected speech – deracinated, phantasmagoric, mellifluous, soporific, interwoven with tidy contra-distinctions and tiny possibilities.

Genteel syntax, of which the subjunctive mood of verbs is a serviceable gauge, is the sword and the shield of the professional, the stratification police of Italian middle-class diction, the invisible dragon waiting to leap from the mouth of every white-collar gallant from Lombardy to Sicily. I'm not envious of these people's command of Italian, I swear. Quite the contrary. English culture until the nineteenth century and Russian culture well into the twentieth were aristocratic in both origin and tone, if anything more partial to the impassioned amateur than to the established academician. Logically, it is the indicative and, even more clearly, the imperative mood of verbs that takes pride of place in my system of cultural values, and it is this level of syntax that, fortuitously, is much the easier on the foreigner's tongue.

An English diarist of the 1990s records that Kingsley Amis liked to tell the story of how he and Anthony Powell once went to tape a literary discussion at the BBC. The producer, a loquacious and eager young man, kept fiddling with the presentation, saying he would like the writers to speak more about this, highlight that, and so on. "We're not interested in the way you would like it," said Powell funereally in what, to my mind, is a perfect parody of genteel syntax in English. "We're only interested in the way we would like it."

The very term, command of language, has something about it that is neither civilian nor very civil. "I would have liked to have done this for you, certainly," says the enlisted man to the commanding officer in a play about Italian life which somebody may one day write, "but unfortunately, due to circumstances which would not have been in my control even if the course of events had shown itself to be something other than it had, I was not able to be of much help in carrying out my ord—, I mean your instructions." This is more or less how the professional gallant uses his education to keep his dignity, by distancing himself from the thing which must be done in order not to become its doer, that is to say a mere servant or subject, and hence something other than perfectly genteel:

> Voglio far il gentiluomo,
> e non voglio più servir,

as the lout Leporello sings in the opening scene of *Don Giovanni*, borrowing, like a nobleman's cloak, his master's indicative mood of the verb "to want."

"I want this." "Give me that." "Do it." This is how a child talks. Or a commanding officer, that is, historically speaking, a nobleman. Or a foreigner like me, straight of purpose as a Moroccan street vendor and bold of desire as an Elizabethan page. I have never cracked an Italian grammar book, and now that my abysmal laziness has found for itself such apposite rationale, somehow I doubt I ever will. Too much grammar is the only thing that's wrong with this country.

XXVI Venice

The Last Doge's English

I now want to add another likeness to my Gogolian gallery of Venice's living souls. If this continuing series should really start to take on the blurry aspect of a spinning carousel, becoming a kind of soap opera of fleeting impressions, all I can say in my defence is that the development is an intended one, and that the clamorous success of Monet's water lilies, for instance, owes far more to the soap effect than does my own humble sketching. Impressionism is a perfectly good approach to the world, but it probably ought not to have fallen into the hands of the French who, like all regicides since Lady Macbeth, long to turn everything under the sun into a *savonnerie*.

And invariably I think of my friend Giovanni as of someone who has managed to escape that perfumed world with his judgement intact, although French remains the language most native to him. Idiomatic as they are, neither his standard Italian nor his deeply Americanized English, which I would describe as heavy-hearted, is good enough to let him say what he really thinks. As for his Venetian – not a minor dialect among Italy's many, but a literary language with a rich tradition that includes the theatre of Carlo Goldoni – it is altogether stillborn, which may be bewildering to the visitor from abroad who finds himself drinking wine and eating roast veal in the house of the man who governed Venice for much of the century, Giovanni's father, Count Giuseppe Volpi di Misurata.

But however serious or trivial the reason for the visitor's bewilderment, the natives themselves have many more such reasons, and are consequently far more perplexed, with the result that asking a Venetian about Giovanni Volpi is as hazardous as walking through a construction site without a helmet on. It is their aggregate reaction, some voluble hybrid of a Nevada filling station attendant talking about Howard Hughes, a retired colonel in Hampshire talking about Bill Gates, and a Gdansk orchestra's concertmaster talking about Herbert von Karajan, that is the focal point of my impressions here.

The long and the short of it is that, to Venice, Giovanni is a mystery. Some of this tenebrous aura is obviously an inheritance from his father, who managed Italy's finances until the war: "Count Volpi is the voice of sincerity," said Mussolini. "He is not afraid of me. He is not afraid of anybody. It could be ventured that he is much more powerful than the head of the fascist regime." The quotation is from *Taccuini Mussoliniani* by Yvon De Begnac, a mammoth, decade-long continuous interview with the Duce, unpublished until the author's death in 1990 and still largely unknown despite the revelations it contains.

Apparently he was the only man in Italy whom the Duce addressed as *lei*. To understand what respect is attached by a dictator to this simple pronoun we may recall that Stalin reserved the polite *vy* for the scourge of Stalingrad, Marshal Zhukov. Mussolini himself, to say nothing of his economic field marshal whom he called "the last Doge," emerges from the book as a complex, independent, and wholly engaging figure, a brave thinker and a good talker:

… who has managed to escape that perfumed world with his judgement intact

His recollections are not of men, but of a city. And for him, Venice is the universal city. If the world became one big Venice, the site of the foremost of human sentiments, he would deem himself a happy man. His melancholy hinges upon the knowledge that this dream can never be realized.

On the crisis of 1929, which, Mussolini says, "Count Volpi was the only European financier to survive unscathed":

> "Waste!" Count Volpi uttered this word a number of times. "Waste, destruction of useful things, overproduction of useless things, people rushing into cities, urbanization, a diminishing desire to work, get-rich-quick mania, gambling away the future, intelligence subjugated to fortune, a middle class turned stupid, and workers resigned to their fate: there's your crisis!"

And on the gestation of Hitler's war, whose deep-hidden Soviet roots are only now beginning to be exposed to historical scrutiny with the publication of works like Stephen Koch's *Double Lives*, Ernst Topisch's *Stalin's War*, and Viktor Suvorov's *Icebreaker* trilogy:

> In the wake of the *Anschluss*, Count Volpi said to me: "Germany is heading towards Moscow, with the Kremlin's consent." Immediately after Munich, he said: "Berlin is moving towards Moscow, offering a morsel to Warsaw. Poland will chew on the morsel, but we all know who will gulp it down."

Such was Giovanni's intellectual inheritance, which he was free to accept as he chose. Yet, naturally, the world being what it is – even this ideal world, locked away in the filigreed lagoon like a portrait miniature in a gold locket, all but hidden from envious magpies and other scavengers of social progress – *le tout Venise* is far more keenly aware of his inheritance of bricks and mortar, including the beautifully preserved sixteenth-century Palazzo Martinengo-Volpi, just up the Canal from Corte Tron where I used to live and where we first met. Giovanni is rarely there, however, preferring to spend his time at Ca' Leone, the family house on the Giudecca that drowns in flowers every spring.

He is not married. People say that he is a recluse, that he loathes their city, that he is never here, that he prefers Paris, that he never goes to parties, that he shuns their company, that he is a snob, a misanthrope, an oddball... And the truth? The truth is that he is a virtuous man, a Venetian to the marrow of his bones, a man who has chosen to accept his intellectual inheritance in its entirety, mixed blessings and all – come hell or *acqua alta* – and, braving the incomprehension, and the uncomprehending scorn, of those who would see Venice merely as a restful alternative to Hollywood and Cannes, a quaint destination for the glamour crowd, has centred his life on solitary scholarship and the study of modern history.

Yet who, even in the ideal world that is Venice, a place that in a most benign sense is something like a century behind the times, can possibly understand why a wealthy bachelor spends his days photocopying documents and poring over book catalogues, when it was his own old man who had started the Venice Film Festival and he could be spending his balmy carefree nights bragging to *décolleté* starlets in tapestried ballrooms by candlelight? As Arkady Belinkov once said, "I testify under oath that there are no circumstances in which the human soul is less immanent than the costliest kind of sausage." Rare indeed are those who would so testify alongside the Russian writer, especially if the casting for the role of the costliest sausage is done the Hollywood way. Certainly none would escape society's ridicule.

Hence, I sometimes think, Giovanni's heavy-hearted American accent when he speaks English, an accent I thought I had never heard, and would almost certainly never have thought of as admirable, until I met him. It is an instinctive way of putting distance between himself and what he sees as the social quagmire of an involuntarily modernizing Italy, something into which his own secretly beloved city must vanish one day. Because not only is the dream of the world becoming one big Venice, prosperous islands in a placid lagoon, not any closer to being realized than in his father's time, but on the contrary, it is more and more like the rest of the gross and turbulent modern world that the universal city cannot avoid becoming.

Now that I think of it, it occurs to me that I have heard that desperately American accent before, the first time from the mouth of a family friend in Moscow who spent many years in Siberian concentration camps. Jack's parents, American Communist Party stalwarts in the 1930s, had lived all their lives in the United States thinking of themselves as Russian and eventually emigrated to the Soviet Union with their teenage son, whereupon all were promptly arrested. Jack used to tell how in his youth in Chicago he would say "Russian!" when asked about his nationality, and how, on the night of their arrest, the question was put to him again in Lefortovo prison. "And I barked back: *Amer-r-ican!*"

The other time I heard it, in a somewhat more comical context, was in a bit of dialogue from Preston Sturges's *Palm Beach Story*, in which Rudy Vallee, playing the reclusive John D. Hackensacker III, meets a dishevelled Claudette Colbert in the sleeping compartment of a train. The next day, after he has bought her a diamond bracelet for each of her new dresses with "bracelet-length sleeves" ("Eet eez all the r-aaah-ge!" exclaims the *vendeuse*), she demands to know why a millionaire should be found travelling by train in anything less grand than a stateroom. "Staterooms," replies Rudy Vallee, "are un-American."

As I said, it is not easy for Venetians to understand why *il Conte* does not spend more time in the Palazzo Volpi. If it were, perhaps he would.

XXVII Venice

About the Tourists

Summer in Venice means tourists. Do I hate them? No more, I assure you, than a patient stricken with a mortal illness hates the individual viral agents, or virions, which are draining the nucleic-synthesizing energy of his body cells to replicate themselves. He hates the disease, which is making him weak, old, and ugly even as he awaits death, but it would take an extraordinarily perverse human mind to revile a faceless submicroscopic particle of the kind first described by my compatriot Dmitry Ivanovsky in 1892 and finally shown to exist by W. M. Stanley in 1935.

We loathe and fear epidemic plagues, evil tyrants with atom bombs, and even fairy-tale ghosts and dragons, because they and their like have left a record of suffering in our collective cultural memory, but the truth is that our emotions simply cannot reach beyond the light stage of the microscope. Imagine asking a grieving widow, who has just lost her husband to swine flu, which characteristic of his killer she finds most repellent. Is it the nucleic composition? Is it the structure of the capsid?

The whole deadly drama of the epidemic that strikes Italy in summertime is the faceless uniformity of the tourist mass. As soon as the patient begins to run a high temperature, hoping to allay the feverish, sweltering afternoon heat by cranking up bar awnings, opening café umbrellas, and hosing down the pavements, millions of faceless virions in white sneakers throng every vessel and swell every node. I have no medical training, and the term "sneakers" is, I am quite certain, a hopelessly obsolete way of describing what the travellers in Europe have on their feet.

All I can say is that these bulky polymer parcels are nearly always white, which, given the variety and abundance of consumer desires, and of technical means for satisfying them, in the United States and elsewhere, is genuinely puzzling. It is as though there existed in the world but a single shade of lipstick, and just one sort of perfume, both manufactured in a factory by the name of Red Moscow. Why not make them black, pink, pomegranate? Why not brand them as Soul Black, Shame Pink, Caprice Red? Perhaps the explanation lies in the fact that tourists in Italy are almost invariably Caucasian, and white people think that so long as they are white, thick plastic foot coverings are elegantly understated. In Russia people used to think that army boots, unless they squeaked, were inconspicuous.

Here is a couple of posters snatched from a fairly expensive hotel in Rome, where I went to meet the conductor Evelino Pidò, down from his native Turin for the season première of *La Traviata* at the Teatro dell'Opera. I was waiting for the maestro at reception with our mutual London friend Didier de C— when my eyes fell on a bulletin board completely covered with dozens of similar announcements. Though mystified and apprehensive, Didier none the less collaborated by diverting the desk's attention while I harvested them in sheaves:

Your Escort: Carrani Incoming s.r.l.

6:45	Wake Up Call
6:30 – 10:00	Breakfast
7:45	Departure St. Peter's for Canonization Mass Meeting in Lobby
	Free Afternoon

Another memorandum, which deals more explicitly with aspects of dress and behaviour, is headed "Your Daily Tour Itinerary LPRL/239":

LONDON, PARIS, ROME

Welcome to Rome!

Friday 28th	Optional: Rome by Night & Dinner. Casual Clothes.
Saturday 29th	Optional: Vatican Museums. Comfortable Clothes but No Shorts.
	Optional: Tivoli Gardens & Dinner. Comfy Shoes, Smart/Casual Wear.
Sunday 30th	Airport.

Your Tour Director: Susan & Veronica.

There you have it, 239 canonization mass meetings in hotel lobbies and comfy shoes, 239 casual afternoons in optional clothes, 239 Romes by Night, and that's only the bookings of a single tour operator, "Trafalgar: The Best in Europe." Multiplied by what, twenty loyal employees of Michigan Catholic Radio? That's 4780, or 9560 sneakered feet. How many Michigan Catholic Radios? How many Trafalgars? Oh, thousands, so we're easily talking of a white sneaker for every man, woman, and child in Italy, a kind of global Imelda Marcos wardrobe, but in reverse, with identical items of footwear as far as the eye can see. No, what am I saying! If they all stood on a single wardrobe shelf, at three sneakered feet to a sneakered metre they would rival the circumference of the globe.

Naturally here in Venice, as everywhere else in Italy and in the rest of tourable Europe, the tourists wear the same-looking jeans, have the same-looking knapsacks on their backs, and eat the same aeroplane food as they approach their destination. When the human virions deviate from their cell-block, uniform norm, it happens as inexplicably as a prison riot on a hot summer's night. For instance, why is it that airlines provide their passengers with metal forks, spoons, and knives when everything else on their folding trays, including of course the food, is made of plastic? Why is it that visitors to the Vatican may not wear shorts, when it is quite clear that the last vestiges of respect and decorum, to say nothing of any more narrowly religious sentiment, were shed by the tourist mass a generation ago? Why is it that Susan and Veronica are not lesbian activists, or at least single mothers?

If one believes as I do that the deadliest disease ever experienced by mankind is totalitarianism, one can only assume that European tourism is yet another of the many ways in which the citizens of Western democracies are preparing themselves, and are being prepared, for this imminent global plague. In *The Decline and Fall of the Roman Empire*, Gibbon wrote of the nonconformist who, in escaping from Rome, could once hope to find

> a secure refuge, a new fortune adequate to his merit, the freedom of complaint, and perhaps the means of revenge. But the empire of the Romans filled the world, and, when that empire fell into the hands of a single person, the world became a safe and dreary prison for his enemies. The slave of Imperial despotism, whether he was condemned to drag his gilded chain in Rome and the senate, or to wear out a life of exile on the barren rock of Seriphus, or the frozen banks of the Danube, expected his fate in silent despair. To resist was fatal, and it was impossible to fly.

In other words, it is not enough that the American should have his hamburgers of prefabricated and frozen offal; he must eat exactly the same prefabricated and frozen offal everywhere in Europe. It is not enough that he should dress like a globetrotting athlete at home, traversing the leafy parking lot of a shopping mall or driving dreamily through a redbrick suburb; for the homogenizing process to be effective, he must wear that same uniform as he scales the bridges of Venice. To resist must be fatal; and it must be impossible to fly.

... canonization mass meetings in hotel lobbies and comfy shoes

XXVIII Forte dei Marmi

Culture for the People

The photographs were commissioned by a music company for the cover of Andrea Bocelli's next cult album. The last one had sold 5,000,000. We were visiting the popular tenor at his house in the resort of Forte dei Marmi, and decided to spend a few days at one of the town's innumerable beach hotels, all equally deserted as the start gun of the Roman holiday stampede had not yet been fired. As he Nikoned away at his subject with a lens the size of a Parma ham ("Cheeky eyes!" he almost demanded at one point, before remembering that the singer is indeed blind), my friend Gusov kept hissing to himself in Russian a 1960s hooligan ditty:

> *Culture for the people,*
> *A store where you shop for free!*

I thought that in the circumstances this too was a bit tactless, but all the same we had a great big elitist cackle about it afterwards.

And then the long journey back to Venice on a hot muggy summer day. I was beginning to feel irritable. Time seemed to stand still, like the hour and minute hands in magazine advertisements for wristwatches, which, gold Patek Philippe or plastic Swatch, are always showing either ten minutes after ten or ten to two. The idea behind this universal convention is that the moment is uniquely flattering to the beauty of the watch face, with which the hands are then in perfect harmony, and one may well ask why anybody needs to have any sort of movement inside in the first place, if this is the way time is supposed to look.

This is a political question, more subversive, in fact, than the question of whether the next president of the United States is an onanist, whether the incumbent is a perjurer and a rapist, or whether the American Constitution should be rewritten once and for all by the faculty of the Yale Law School. If I had the technical and financial means to bring it to the attention of the American people that George Bush, like his father, began his adult life with a ritual sacrifice of Christian dignity to opportunistic careerism, I am convinced that he would not "get to be president." By contrast, a simple convention, such as that upon which the commercial success of a blind tenor, or of a Swiss chronometer, is hinged, is practically unchallengeable, based as it is on centuries of cultural conditioning, ethical as well as aesthetic.

Consider for a moment the convention of the ordinary mirror. When a woman inspects herself in a glass, she wishes to see herself as others would see her, and only a psychologically insensible observer will tell you that her expectation or purpose is any different. And yet it ought to be perfectly plain to the woman that her wish is one hundred percent unattainable, that what the glass is reflecting is how she sees herself, that and that alone. Why bother with mirrors then? And yet

… the last one had sold 5,000,000

they are ineradicable, as much part of the mise-en-scène of our civilization as time and language, music and painting, oil and wine.

In Florence I had to change trains again, and as the Eurostar on which I had a reservation was simply not there I had to choose whether to kill time chatting to prostitutes outside the station or looking at postcards displayed in the kiosks. The postcards were all of Michelangelo's David. I counted fourteen slightly different versions. By a strange coincidence, when I finally did board the train, there was on my seat a copy of *The Times*, left there by some absentminded Englishman, with a front-page photograph of the Florentine landmark. "Michelangelo's David," read the caption: "The squint means the eyes look beautiful on both profiles."

The story was that a Stanford University research team, having laser-scanned the head of the marble sculpture, determined that Michelangelo's hero is cross-eyed, apparently "on purpose, because it provided good profiles of David when seen from either side." Naturally, as the sculpture is gigantic, nobody had ever noticed this before, and in my growing irritation I had to ask the obvious, tactless, Russian question, namely, if realism was the confessed aim of the Renaissance, how come they made their sharpshooter cross-eyed? And what gave them the idea to make their David the size of Goliath?

Culture for the people,
A store where you shop for free!

I have already written here, during what I now recall as my years of Florentine captivity, about the parallels between the Renaissance of the Medici and the socialist realism of my native land's recent past. The theme is a vast one, and while its chilling depths hold an attraction for me that is almost hypnotic, what might have remained a private obsession has been dilated and rendered objective by readings in such intellectually disciplined prophets of the universal totalitarian tomorrow as Vasily Rozanov and Pavel Florensky.

I cannot describe Rozanov as the greatest writer Russia has ever produced because, as he himself once wrote, to speak of a writer's stature is as idiotic as to compare Joan of Arc with a railroad. Suffice it to say that I believe that Rozanov is to the twenty-first century what Dostoevsky has been proved by the twentieth, while Father Florensky, who incidentally administered his philosopher friend's last rites at his death from cold and hunger in 1919, may be described as that balancing intellectual force of counter-reformation which the West has been wanting so pitifully since at least the invention of moveable type. No Modern Convention, no Liberal Premise, no Child of Enlightenment is safe, thank goodness, so long as a single page of their writings remains unincinerated and unsuppressed.

Take Darwin, for a more or less relevant example. "Darwin never noticed," wrote Rozanov,

that in nature the eyes glisten. He has depicted nature as opaque, with extinguished, dead eyes... He has created filth, not zoology. And the filthy epoch has bowed to his filth: "We don't need music, we've got the gramophone." Such is Darwinism.

"The mouth is for eating." Fine, wonderful. But all you need for that is an orifice through which "food is introduced." Instead, the mouth is not an orifice, but – a mouth. "A lovely mouth." Perhaps, as I think, for kissing? No? Why not? It is uniquely human that the mouth should be so beautiful, which is why no other animal likes to kiss. While the one whose love begins with a kiss has been given a uniquely beautiful mouth.

The reader can confirm for himself the truth of Rozanov's sentiments by gazing for half an hour, as I did on that train spiriting me away from the cradle of Western humanism, into the dead eyes of Michelangelo's David, those vacant half-globes of marble with holes at their centres that are meant to look, from a great distance and only to a spectator positioned more or less directly beneath, like the Biblical hero's pupils. If Darwin were God, all men would look like Michelangelo's David from a great distance.

Uncovering the actual roots of Renaissance art in the theatre design of ancient Greece and of the Roman *graeculorum*, Florensky analysed both its illusionist, pyrotechnic, crowd-pleasing aims and its assumption of a captive and immobile, politically paralysed audience with similar mercilessness:

> The pathos of the modern man is in ridding himself of all reality, whereupon his naked "I want" would legislate over a new reality entirely of his own construction, phantasmagoric though clearly expressible on graph paper. The pathos of the ancient as well as the mediaeval man is, to the contrary, in the grateful acceptance of every reality, for all being is goodness and all goodness – being. The pathos of the mediaeval man is in the affirmation of the reality within and without him; hence objectivity. While modern subjectivism invites illusionism, nothing could be further away from the intentions and thoughts of the man of the Middle Ages than creation of appearances and life among fictions.

I want to end this with a kind of *diminuendo* flourish, which seems apt and more than a little funny. My friend Gusov rang up a few weeks ago, to report that he had spoken with a woman from the recording company. "I asked them what they thought of the Bocelli photos," he said, already chuckling in anticipation. "'He is delighted!' the woman said. I said, 'How do you mean, *he* is delighted?… I mean, he is…' 'Well,' said the woman, 'you know what I mean. His *manager* is delighted.'" And then, again, hissing into the phone, that leitmotif of our Forte dei Marmi days:

Culture for the people,
A store where you shop for free!

XXIX Rieti

Good Help Nowadays

I start this story not at my own desk in the Palazzo Mocenigo, but in a hammock suspended between two graceful pine trees in a place called Oliveto, up in the Sabine Hills, an hour's drive from Rome. The settlement of a dozen houses is dominated by the Villa Parisi, a mediaeval *casale* set in a large hillside garden, which some friends from London have taken for a week's stay. The nearest big town, with a population of 45,830, according to the *44esima edizione della Guida Michelin* found in the rented car, is Rieti, but I did not come here to fret about sightseeing in Northern Lazio. I came here to make jokes, play cards, sleep, drink, and talk about the servants. In England there is a name for this kind of summer divertissement, which is supposed to take place somewhere beyond the confines of the former Empire, usually in Greece, Spain, or Italy. It is called a villa holiday.

Of course the arrangements have been made through a London agency, which knows as much about Italy as the Moscow correspondent of the *New York Times* knows about Russia, and – if such a monster can be imagined – is even more defensively verbose. Accordingly, once the promised luxuries have been paid for in advance, the tenants receive a descriptive folder of several hundred pages, complete with slightly inaccurate maps and wholly imaginary menus, which boils down to something like this: "Just bring your own bloody towels, buy your own bloody Scotch, stay on the bloody terrace, and for Heaven's sake don't bother the servants. They are foreign, and we don't know what they're saying." Consequently what we are given here is the kitchen equivalent of a movie star's autobiography, which may be just as well. Like Byron in Venice, I worry about getting fat.

What do I tell my English friends about the servant problem? That there is a reason why I fell for their idea of the villa holiday, apart from the pleasure of seeing them. Our Stakhanovite nanny and housekeeper of four years, Sandra, who had come with us from London to Rome, and later to Venice, handed in her resignation a few weeks ago. In London she once chased away an *Evening Standard* reporter, who thought he would take a sentimental photograph of my son playing among the daffodils in Hyde Park, with a softly-spoken Russian phrase that means "I'll rip your mouth." In Rome, asked what she thought of the Italians, she answered: "They are a noisy and shameless people." It was in Venice that this loyal, hard-working, and God-fearing woman was finally corrupted, and of course it would be hypocritical to blame her. The purple-pink light of the setting sun reflecting off the stone façades of the Giudecca is more or less clearly unsuited to the task of vacuuming a child's bedroom. Like me, poor Sandra realized that what she really wanted was to sit in the café all day and drink Aperol spritzers, and that this great pleasure actually cost very little.

The corruption takes hold of the victim in slow increments, Italian life as a whole only too ready to supply an object lesson at every step. "*Buon giorno, Signora!*" It would never occur to the

... a leading fishmonger in the Rialto market

average Russian of Sandra's generation, the last to graduate from Stalin's university of life, to comment on the weather to a total stranger. "For that *we* have meteorologists. Ah, you beg to differ? Then you're probably a Trotskyist spy." It would never occur to us to address a maid as Madame. "What's that you're playing at? Bourgeois egalitarianism? In *our* country people are shot for less." Indeed, it has taken the death of a hundred million of our countrymen to teach the other 100 million to mind their business, so it would seem that the very least I can count on there, by way of personal benefit, is a good maid.

But eventually the bonhomie routine grinds down the toughest Stakhanovite, and she dissolves in all that wretched civility like a *baicolo* biscuit. Before you know it, she is no longer an anodized-steel bolt holding together an infinitesimal part of a vast statist machine – such as the employer's household – but a vulgar Western chatterbox, a nosy know-it-all with a diversity of subjective preoccupations, a "wicked and slothful servant" labouring in the belief that disobedience is a substitute for talent. She has become a person, a citizen, a god.

If individual talent is, as I believe, the only acceptable excuse for democratic delusions of this kind, then Margarita, our cook, represents the Western ideal. Margarita speaks only dialect, with the consequence that when she wants to express the most basic thought – even one so proverbially simple as "to each his own" – something altogether gorgeous and outlandish, like the San Marco cathedral, emerges from her island brain. "*Ghe xe queó,*" she says, rolling up her sleeves to plunge a pair of powerful arms into the colourful chaos of a postprandial sink, "*che ghe piase ciuciár el caenasso,*" meaning, "some people like to lick a lock." We all adore her, a Venetian to the marrow of her soup bones, in part because her Italian is as bad as ours.

I met her through her husband, a leading fishmonger in the Rialto market who had already won our not inconsiderable custom. Then one day my friend Alberto brought over a dozen wild ducks he had shot, still in feather. With that millstone around my neck, in pouring rain – it was some time before the Madonna della Salute, and unless you are a hunter the weather is terrible – I made fruitless rounds of Venice's butchers, hoping to get them plucked at any price, until finally I came to the Rialto and saw Beppe in his white apron, presiding over his *banco*. Before I could finish my tale of woe, he swept all the fish remains before him into the gutter with a majestic stroke of a giant blade and, with the same gracefully curved movement, cut the tie that bound the birds together.

It was a kind of European Community nightmare. Feathers flew as far as the eye could see, drifting flirtatiously over the snowy banks of bass and sole. Under the roof of the covered market a crowd gathered, Venetians and *foresti* in equal numbers. The foreigners spoke in hushed undertones among themselves, lamenting the barbarity of a country that allows meat and fish to be handled on the same premises. The natives were louder, but more curious than incensed: "What's that you're doing?" they would ask. "Oh, nothing," Beppe would reply, relishing the conflict between the individual and the mass, "just some new kind of octopus I got in. With feather on 'em." When, some months later, Beppe offered us a Venetian as a cook, all he said by way of recommendation was that she is his wife. Or maybe he offered us his wife as a cook and said, by way of recommendation, that she is Venetian.

There is a story about Byron, which I think Peter Quennell dug up while researching the circumstances of his life at the Palazzo Mocenigo, involving a local type reminiscent of our own Margarita. "La Fornarina," the baker's wife who became the poet's mistress and later his housekeeper, once snatched off the mask of a noblewoman who happened at that moment to have accepted Byron's arm. When he later reproached her, explaining that Madame Contarini is a lady, she snapped back: "She may be a lady, but I am a Venetian!" How well that defiant *mi son Venexiana!* would sit on our beloved Margarita's lightly moustachioed lips. No wonder Byron worried about his weight.

Margarita took over the household until Sandra's replacement could arrive from Moscow. It quickly turned out that the selfsame qualities that made her a legend in our kitchen – her innovative boldness bordering on recklessness, her open disdain for everything with a printed label, her fierce sense of independence – were grossly counterproductive in a maid. *Mi son Venexiana!* In a week's time the house was laid waste, with that morning-after feeling about it, as if somebody had tearfully pleaded with a couple of bachelors not to trash the place. Plants killed, papers missing, books moved, ashtrays full, laundry dirty, the electric iron broken, Beppe watching football in the kitchen, Margarita's daughter sunbathing on the terrace, and Margarita herself nowhere to be seen. "Do not ask Chaliapine to represent you in court, demur if Cicero offers to sing for you, and never assume that a talented cook will make a dutiful housekeeper," was how I finished telling the story to my friends at the Villa Parisi.

The following Sunday I was at the Marco Polo airport to collect Vera. There is a moment on the way back, once the boat enters Venice and crawls out into the Grand Canal at Ca' d'Oro, that is so absurdly unforgettable that I, not content to relive it daily in the freeze-frame of my own window, seize every opportunity to go to the airport just to experience it afresh. And there I was, watching Vera next to me, Vera who had never been out of Russia, Vera about to collide, at five kilometres an hour, with the absurdly unforgettable moment, watching her and thinking, "Well? Well? What will she say?"

Nothing. She never even looked up once. The Grand Canal is none of her business. She is the Stakhanovite maid I want.

XXX Capri

What Epimenides Said

Among the unaccountable peculiarities of this diary, and indeed of my general way of seeing things, is that one can never expect to learn something of Capri from my impressions of Capri. And yet, I keep asking as though to placate myself, why should it be otherwise? I am aboard the *Stamos* with a group of friends who foregathered at a beachfront villa in Sabaudia and then sailed the 90-ft catamaran – built by our host, who financed the French team, as an observation vessel for the America's Cup race some years back – to Ponza, Ischia, and Capri. I don't know anything about sailing apart from the Dutch naval terms that entered the Russian language at the time of Peter the Great. I don't know any more about the Amalfi Coast than any sunburnt accountant who has ever eaten the *insalata caprese* or appeased his girlfriend with a pair of Capri pants in cerulean cotton twill. The sea is blue and warm, obviously. The coast, as anyone who has seen the Bay of Naples on the wall of a pizzeria can recall, is rocky and picturesque. The mozzarella is delicious, and the girls are buxom. So, what is there to say?

Besides, my mind is back in Venice, where I just learned that our landlady at the Palazzo Mocenigo, the young *contessa* with the lawyer whose verbs are always in a mysterious mood, does not intend to renew our lease when it expires in the autumn. I now need to find another place to live, one that would be cheap enough not to alienate myself in the affections of friends yet grand enough to strike fear in the hearts of enemies, one that would be beautiful enough to spin tales about yet modern enough to have central heating. As there are precisely 221 buildings on the Grand Canal, and fewer than half are in private hands, the task of finding an apartment to satisfy these modest demands is formidable even from the point of view of simple statistics. But, as so often in life and always at roulette, in actual fact the problem is less statistical than it is dramatic.

A neighbour at the Mocenigo was away in Apulia this summer. One day, when the tanned and rested Signor A— returned to Venice to check up on things back home, he saw scaffolding on his balcony. The management of the palazzo, whom he had been petitioning for some years to make some repairs to the exterior, had finally brought the masons round but apparently neglected to tell him about the scheduled works. Concluding at once that the scaffolding had not been put up with the delicacy owed to the historic importance of his ancestral home, right then and there he suffered a heart attack. He is still in hospital. But the gruesome punch line is that during the previous decade Signor A— had outlived, and buried, both of his sons, young men of great charm and ability, without any appreciable harm to his famously robust constitution. Losing both one's children in their prime, and looking none the less tanned and rested for it, is quite normal in this social environment. Losing some plaster curlicues on the front of your house is a different matter entirely.

... the management neglected to tell him about the works

I am convinced that back in 1851, at the world première of Verdi's *Rigoletto* at the Fenice – with Teresa Brambilla as Gilda, Raffale Mirate as the Duke, and Felice Varesi as Rigoletto – the audience applauded the new opera because, subconsciously, every Venetian interpreted the hero's madly possessive love for his daughter as an allegory of his own private feelings about his corporeal hereditament, meaning his house and all its movable heirlooms. "*La donna è... mobili!*" they probably thought, that's right, at last somebody's said it, a woman is just like that fine pair of ormolu commodes I stand to inherit from my aunt. "*Questa o quella?*" sang the dissolute Duke, choosing the object of his seductive attentions, but the audience probably saw an unscrupulous foreigner ogling their palazzi on the Grand Canal ("What if it was *your* house?!"). And so on down to the final scene, in which the hero discovers his daughter felled by the vengeful blow he had sought to direct at her presumed seducer:

> Gilda! Mia Gilda!.. È morta!…
> Ah, la maledizione!
> (*Strappandosi i capelli, cade sul cadavere della figlia.*)

Ah, the curse! (And, tearing at his hair, he falls upon the breathless body.) This is just how a Venetian of ancient lineage feels about the unforeseen outcome of a quarrel with an intransigent plumber, or an avaricious plasterer. *Miei pavimenti!* My floors! (Only a barely audible creaking by way of reply.) *Miei stucchi!* My ceiling reliefs! (Waterlogged.) *Le cose della mamma!* Mommy's things! (Sold at auction by the wastrel uncle.) Because the truth, which every charlatan beginning with Freud has made a living obfuscating, is that any human trait can work backwards as well as forwards. While a Viennese psychiatrist may well want to sleep in his mother's canopied bed because it reminds him of his mother, a Venetian gentleman is far more likely to want to sleep with his mother because she reminds him of her canopied bed.

Given such intensity of natural feeling, suggesting that it may be rather easier to check into a Three-Star Kraut Excelsior & Rooms in Mantua with the virgin Gilda under the name of "Mr. & Mrs. P. Rubirosa" than to honourably rent her father's apartment in Venice on a one-year, tourist-accommodation lease, it is hardly surprising that when I look at a piazza in Rome, a street in Milan, or as now a stretch of the Amalfi coastline, all I can really see is so much easily rentable, emotionally neutral lodging. The house on the Grand Canal, or more specifically the filet-mignon portion of it called the *piano nobile*, is all the Venetian *nobil homo* has in this world. It is the habitation of his dignity. To him, the house is a machine for feeling.

An added complication is that Venice – though more cosmopolitan, both by tradition and in actual fact, than all the rest of the great Italian cities – is a small town where everybody knows everything about everyone else, and literally none of it is ever remotely true. I say this advisedly. As a Russian I am used to treating rumour and gossip as alternative channels of information, more trustworthy, if anything, than official news bulletins and press reports. As it happens, the local paper, *Il Gazzettino*, has just astonished Venice with the news that the American owner of the Palazzo Persico, directly across the Grand Canal from the Mocenigo, "rents out" – has rented?

would rent? is thinking of renting? has had a dream in which she was going to rent? Italian syntax goes all coy at this juncture – "her *piano nobile* for $60,000 a month." From this one may easily draw the mistaken conclusion that no rumour, and no gossip, can possibly be as false as what gets printed in newspapers.

In my childhood we laughed at the question of whether it was true that a certain Armenian had won a million in the state lottery. The answer was: "Yes, it is true. But it wasn't in the state lottery, it was at cards, and it wasn't a million, it was a hundred roubles, and he didn't win, he lost." Whether the nice Mrs. P— rents out her apartment for $60,000, or $6000, or $600 a month, there is still at least an element of truth in the *Gazzettino* story, whereas the things one hears at dinner at the Circolo, the gentlemen's club where the city elders doze over their Camparis, are total, blinding, byzantine inventions that run, roughly, as follows.

"Countess M— has run off with a Colombian drug baron. The Count has eczema, caused, I happen to know, by a bad oyster he once ate in Monte Carlo. Later this year he will be going to Switzerland for prolonged specialist treatment. You should speak to his nephew in Milan, who is an important publisher of books on the history of dance, and he will almost certainly let you have the apartment." Now the truth is that the nephew, a banker in New York, has not been to Italy since the age of three; that it was back in 1959 that the Countess left her husband for an English race-car driver; and that the 82-year-old Count, eczema or no eczema, is happily ensconced in his ancestral palazzo in the company of a raven-haired Brazilian dancer named Miu, whom he has found through an Internet singles site. By the time you've unravelled the knot and followed up the lead, the old man drowns in his bath, Miu turns blonde, and the apartment is rented to a RAI television executive.

Byzantine indeed. "The worst," as Byron noted of the people of Greece in whose service he was about to lay down his life,

> is that (to use a course but the only expression that will not fall far short of the truth) they are such damned liars; there never was such an incapacity for veracity shown since Eve lived in Paradise. One of them found fault the other day with the English language, because it had so few shades of a Negative, whereas a Greek can so modify a "No" to a "Yes" and *vice versa*, by the slippery qualities of his language, that prevarication may be carried to any extent and still leave a loop-hole…. This was the gentleman's own talk, and is only to be doubted because in the words of the syllogism "Now Epimenides was a Cretan."

I suppose the moral of the story is that after a year or two at the Palazzo Mocenigo a man should go off and fight for Greek independence, especially if his lease has run out.

XXXI Venice

The Visitors

The first chill of autumn, which reminds us locals to order firewood from the mainland for our illegal fireplaces, is always a moment of reckoning. Not for nothing does the Russian Aesop, Krylov, in his fable of the socially responsible ant and the bohemian dragonfly, suggest that such a moment has arrived when a wintry blast gets in the eyes of the homeless idealist. In my own case, however, the fault is not entirely mine. It seems ages since I started looking for a new apartment, and ages since I began rehearsing the many explanations – some more interesting than "Well, you know, you have to pay the rent…" – of the difficulty of finding one. Last time I described what it's like to try and wrest an apartment from a born-and-bred Venetian. Now I'd like to suggest what happens when the owner of the house is a Venetian by adoption.

Let us unfold a little pocket scenario that involves a socially well-connected visitor to Italy, with a cast of mind typical of what was once called the Fifth Avenue matron. Her daughter, who was at Brown, is an active supporter of Save Venice and has written about it in her alumni notes. Her younger brother, an antiques dealer in the Fulham Road in London, has just got back from Nencia Corsini's wedding in Florence. Her husband, Mr. Matron, is an investment banker from Short Hills, New Jersey. They travel to Europe several times a year, know Italians with residences in Manhattan and Mayfair, have been to charity balls at the Palazzo Pisani Moretta, are used to staying at the Cipriani, and are known by name to the waiters at Harry's Bar. Now they've bought a palazzo of their own, part of which they are thinking of letting to referenced tenants. And here she is, just as she might appear in *W*, "Mrs. Matron in Valentino," in the Sala del Maggior Consiglio of the Ducal Palace, standing inquisitively before the famous black square substituting for the portrait of Marino Falier, with the inscription: HIC EST LOCUS MARINI FALETHRI DECAPITATI PRO CRIMINIBUS. Of the seventy-six Doges represented here, only Falier's face is deleted for all eternity, for the alleged act of treason which got him beheaded in 1355.

Now, the Falier have all died out in the last century, but the Palazzo Falier Canossa – now Palazzo Matrón? – still stands on the Grand Canal, a witness to the family's history. Paolo Lucio Anafesto Falier was elected Doge in Eraclea with the consent of Byzantium, followed by the family's three properly Venetian Doges: Vitale, who built St. Mark's basilica in its final form, Ordelaffo, who founded the shipyards of the Arsenale, and the unfortunate Marino. The story, as told by the chronicler Marin Sanudo, is that during a banquet at the Ducal Palace given by the seventy-year-old Doge and his young wife Alvica Gradenigo, a young "new patrician" by the name of Michele Steno "made a nuisance of himself," whereupon the Doge had him ejected. As he was leaving, Steno made a slanderous proclamation about the woman's virtue, whereupon he was arrested, tried, and sentenced to one month's imprisonment. The Doge, interpreting the lightness of the sentence as a sign that his position was being undermined, conspired against Steno and the party of new patricians which supported him. The plot was discovered, the Doge was beheaded, and all official records of the affair were destroyed. Alvica went mad and spent the rest of her life in seclusion.

What I relish imagining is Falier popping back into this world, suitcase in hand, through that famous black square. Obviously he needs an apartment to rent, at least until he can get his bearings, and at the new Venetian home of Mr. and Mrs. F. A. Matron there ensues the following brutal discussion:

MRS. MATRON: Who's who? I mean, how d'you do? So nice to meet you.

MARINO FALIER: I heard through the grapevine that you have a *piano nobile* I could have on a year's lease. Is that true?

MRS. MATRON: Would you like some coffee? (Rings for the Filipino.) Arthur, will you bring in the coffee, please. Do you know the Sammartini?

MARINO FALIER: Well, as you may have realized during your stroll through the Sala del Maggior Consiglio, I'm not acquainted with very many people after the fateful year 1355. But naturally I can provide you with all the necessary banking references. And, as Doge…

MRS. MATRON (impatiently): I know all that. But the Sammartini own Palazzo Pisani Moretta! We've been to some wonderful parties there, with all those flaming candles, and music, and gondolas… Jenny is a good friend. She is a fantastic decorator.

MARINO FALIER: My ancestor, Vitale…

MRS. MATRON: I'm afraid that name doesn't mean anything to me.

MARINO FALIER: Vitale consecrated St. Mark's. Doesn't that say something about our family's appetite for splendour? And a later ancestor, Ordelaffo, brought the Pala d'Oro to St. Mark's from Constantinople. It is probably the most famous decorative object in the world, with jewels *en cabochon*…

MRS. MATRON: I know all that. But did you attend the wedding of the young Princess Corsini, in Florence? Everybody was there, and it's going to be in *Chi* magazine.

MARINO FALIER: You must pause to reflect that the social world of which you are speaking is alien to me. When my ancestor Anafesto was enthroned, *Chi* magazine did not exist. Florence didn't exist. Since then the one hundred and twenty Doges of Venice, ending with the traitor Lodovico Manin who handed our country over to the French, came from just fifty-nine families. Fifty-nine families in a thousand years. What do we care about princes and princesses? To us, the names to be revered belonged to those who freed Venice from Byzantium: Corner, Ipato, Bembo, Contarini, Morosini, Dandolo, Tiepolo, Gradenigo, Falier… All right, also people like Querini, Zorzi, Soranzo, Ziani, who later joined them. Then came the new patricians, and even though they proved to be my own undoing, I accept those among them who were inscribed in the Golden Book at the close of the Great Council in 1297: Foscari, Loredan, Grimani, Barbarigo, Donà, Gritti, Marcello, Malipiero, Tron, Venier, Mocenigo… We could all have made ourselves princes and marquesses and counts and whatnot, but the only title a Venetian citizen may bear as properly his own is that of *Nobil Homo*. We used to believe this an appellation greater than that of many a king, and even three centuries after my birth Henry III of France, the last Valois, asked that he might be permitted to style himself a Venetian nobleman…

MRS. MATRON: I know all that, but now you expect to live in my… in your palazzo, and I'm not prepared… and frankly puzzled, because you're not really telling me anything. Do you know the Gradenigo family? My brother was staying at their house in the country last weekend. He was at Harvard with Giovanni. And Lucy, I hear, is a wonderful tennis player.

MARINO FALIER: My wife is of the family of Pietro Gradenigo. He became Doge in 1289.

MRS. MATRON: But do you *know* them? I mean, do they *know* you?

MARINO FALIER: Er, well, my name, yes, but I'm afraid…

MRS. MATRON (businesslike): I'll have to speak with my husband, but I don't think we'll be renting out the apartment after all. I'm very sorry to have to cut this short, and it was a pleasure meeting you, but my daughter and I are going to an important meeting of Save Venice this afternoon and I must get ready. It's being held at the home of the Steno family. I was told their ancestor Michele became Doge, too. Do you know them?

MARINO FALIER (killing her with an ornamental paperweight): Aargh!

As the curtain falls on my little vaudeville, I must add a couple of things. One is that almost all the living personages depicted therein are almost entirely my own spiteful inventions. The other is that of course I'm not Marino Falier returned from the dead, but in fact a reasonably eager and even accomplished social climber who would have Mrs. Matron, were I ever to run across such a perfectly formed representative of her social class, eating out of my hand. You want names, babycakes? I give you names. You want country weekends? You can have all the country weekends you want, those golden *week-ends* with a hyphen. You want hobnobbing with princes? Okay, here goes. Unfortunately, life is not vaudeville, and a perfectly formed representative of that social class is hard to find, which leaves me with Mrs. Matron's imperfectly formed, flawed, partial namesakes: German, French, Hungarian, English.

All of them, each in his or her own cluelessly snobbish way, manage to re-enact the scene from the Tenth Canto of Dante's *Inferno*, when the old Ghibelline, Farinata degli Uberti, fixes the poet with his beady eye and demands to know, literally, who in hell he is:

Com' io al piè della sua tomba fui,

    guardommi un poco, e poi, quasi sdegnoso,

    mi dimandò: "Chi fuor li maggior tui?"

Io ch'era d'ubidir disideroso,

    non lil celai, ma tutto lil'apersi…

And the harder I try to "conceal nothing and reveal all," the sorrier I feel for poor Marino Falier. *He* would never find an apartment in Venice.

…when my ancestor Anafesto was enthroned, *Chi* did not exist

XXXII Venice

The Pavlovian Sandwich

Giovanni and I were both in Milan for the day, and he asked me to join him for lunch at Bice with a friend of his, Lauren Bacall. The expensive restaurant was quite empty, we drank a good bit, and the conversation ranged from the actress's favourite *New Yorker* cartoon to the particulars of life in Venice. Then obliquely, in a stage whisper, for the most part inside my own mildly alcoholized brain, it went on to the mercurial ways of glamour and money, and this was what I continued to think about after we'd said our good-byes, all the way back to Venice Santa Lucia. *The father rabbit, seeing off his son at the station, hands him a small package, saying: "Your mother wanted you to have this for luck. It's her foot."* That was the cartoon.

As for life in Venice, we got onto the subject when Miss Bacall dreamily recalled the finger sandwiches that used to be served on aeroplanes in the old days, when transcontinental air travel began to edge out the railways. It was quickly established that the nearest thing going today is the *tramezzino*, and at that point Miss Bacall – I do not chide her, it's just the way people think – added, blithely, "at Harry's Bar." Now, the truth is that the *tramezzino* is as fundamentally Venetian as pizza is Neapolitan, with the consequence that every bar in town makes a sandwich at least as amazing, and ten times cheaper, as what is on offer at the Cipriani establishment. The tuna-and-tomato at the Rosa Salva in Campo S. Luca, for instance, is a minor masterpiece that stems from the same creative source as the comedy of Carlo Goldoni and the music of Benedetto Marcello.

"NO-O-O!?" said Miss Bacall, as if I had just told her that money grows on trees in Giovanni's garden on the Giudecca.

As I say, it's just the way people think. A person has certain clusters of associations in his head, and much of what he sees, even when he sees it with his very own eyes, tends to cling like wet snow to this or that long existing nucleus, rather than to conglobe afresh, spontaneously and capriciously. It is as though there is a snowman of sensibilities being made inside the brain, complete with coals for the eyes and a carrot nose, and the more one witnesses and experiences, the bigger the snowman gets, without ever changing its recognizable contours. So in Miss Bacall's case, for example, the glamour of a flight to Los Angeles, in the days of her youth, adheres more easily to the waiters' jackets and starched tablecloths at Harry's Bar than to the greater Venice of unwashed tourist masses and the cheap cafes that presumably cater to them.

Consider the notion which I am tempted to regard in political terms, fresh orange juice. (If the idea of a great five-cent cigar, or of a chicken in every pot, or of Scotch whisky on every secret-police chief's table can gain acceptance as a political symbol, I fail to see why my example should seem frivolous.) Now, Italy is the only place in the world where asking for a glass of orange juice – at any restaurant or bar, anywhere in Italy, at any time of day – means being given what has just been squeezed into the glass with the contractual aim of filling it, at room temperature, with the juice of fresh oranges. In England or the United States, by contrast, this notion – encompassing though it does a technologically uncomplicated process, squeezing, and a widely available commodity, oranges – belongs to the billionaire world of private jets, of terraces overlooking the ocean, of butlers, mistresses, and scandalous love triangles. Yet even the *Hello!* ambiance is no guarantee. An American billionaire I once stayed with in Beverly Hills, in a house poised above the cascading tiers of a vast orange grove, drank orange juice made from frozen concentrate at breakfast.

The point is that in Italy people do not think less of the luxuries that cost little. Alistair McAlpine, an acquaintance of mine in Venice who has amassed world-class collections of everything from antique beads to farm machinery, once told me that while the tiger cowrie mollusc has the most beautiful shell in the world, it is the far less splendid shell of the *Cypraea moneta* which circulated as a currency among the primitive peoples of the Pacific. Imagine selling a magnificent specimen of the *Cypraea tigris* for a handful of those dull cowries, or swapping a bag of oranges for a can of concentrate, or gold for paper! How paradoxical, and yet, knowing that the perversity of man is only matched by his credulity, how utterly plausible.

It seems to me that so long as the Italians continue to treat luxury as a specimen in a vast and serious collection illustrating the morphological diversity of life, they will not be overrun by money as other nations have been. Because not only is money not the key, it is often a barrier to luxury, as witness the story of an Italian friend who went to stay at the Cala di Volpe in Sardinia, now owned by an American hotel chain and catering to those who, as the shrewd Arabic saying goes, "do not know the taste of their mouth." In the sumptuously appointed lobby there is a long bar, dotted here and there with cash registers. These emit a distinctive whirring sound when operated, which they nearly always are, and this sound, my friend averred, is as quickly rooted in the hotel guest's consciousness as Pavlov's bell is in the salivation of the experimental dog.

"I want a drink" – "Here you are, sir" – *pfrrrr*, $49.50 – "I want a boat for the day" – "The boat is waiting, sir" – *pfrrrrr*, $6,905.00 – "I want a woman for the evening" – "*Eccoci qua, Signore, la bella Svetlana!*" – *pfrrrrr*, $3,999.95 – and so on, until checkout time. On his first night in his room, as he was luxuriating in his grandiose, canopied bed, it occurred to him to turn over and luxuriate on his side, but then – *pfrr*! – he decided against it. He stayed put, flat on his back. "I swear to you," said my friend, "it was demonic. The very instant the desire to turn over took hold of me, straight away I could hear those registers whirring."

Let me restate my case. A terrible conundrum of our bourgeois civilization is whether money can buy happiness. I think it cannot be solved in one go, just as an advanced theorem of geometry cannot be proved by a pupil unfamiliar with the basic principles of Euclidian reasoning. An intermediate question to ponder, in this case, is whether money can buy ordinary comfort, such as the psychological freedom to turn in your bed any which way you please. The answer is, not always. A more advanced question is whether money can buy luxury, glamour, splendour, and here I point to Italy which, quietly but stubbornly, whispers no.

Brescia, then Verona sped by, then Padua. I kept looking out the window of my train, a grimy InterCity originating in Zurich, thinking how odd it was that nobody at Bice made a fuss over my iconic vis-à-vis, that no woman came over squealing some Italian equivalent of "Oh, Miss Bacall,

I just wanted to say, I saw you at the Academy Awards, and I'm so happy, my daughter was doing a lot of acting at Princeton last year, and I just wanted to say, I hope you don't mind my coming up like this, I think you're great, just great, and..." In 1867, on his way from Milan to Venice, Mark Twain recorded passing through the same

> old towns, wedded to the customs and steeped in the dreams of the elder ages, and perfectly unaware that the world turns round! And perfectly indifferent, too, as to whether it turns around or stands still. *They* have nothing to do but eat and sleep and sleep and eat, and toil a little when they can get a friend to stand by and keep them awake. *They* are not paid for thinking – *they* are not paid to fret about the world's concerns.

And yet, he concluded with unconcealed envy, "in their breasts, all their stupid lives long, resteth a peace that passeth understanding! How can men, calling themselves men, consent to be so degraded and happy?"

The answer, as I say, is in the Italian attitude to life's luxuries that is still in evidence today, the degraded and happy attitude that – at least in the green backwater of Venice for which I was headed – still resists the global Pavlovian training intended to link glamour with money. A wisely and freshly made sandwich, however cheap, is a greater luxury than a foolishly cut suit of clothes, however fancy the designer; freshly squeezed juice is the best thing to be had at breakfast, whether or not it is associated with swimming pools and movie stars; and a home-cooked Sunday lunch for twenty, all cousins and aunts from as far afield as Verona and Padua, is more glamorous than the veal escalope at Bice, however famous my luncheon companion and whether the world turns round.

> It was a long, long ride. But toward evening, as we sat silent and hardly conscious of where we were – subdued into that meditative calm that comes so surely after a conversational storm – someone shouted –
>
> "VENICE!"
>
> And sure enough, afloat on the placid sea a league away, lay a great city, with its towers and domes and steeples drowning in a golden mist of sunset.

... afloat on the placid sea a league away, lay a great city

XXXIII Venice

The Women's Movement

After an uninterrupted spell of a winter month or two here in Venice – all footsteps in the evening mist, and quiet conversation about the best way to cook pheasant, and a Neapolitan card game called seven and a half – what one notices on arriving in London is the way women move. First of all, it's the speed. Within the most madamed, to say nothing of pompadoured, porcelain leafiness of Chelsea and Knightsbridge, one is suddenly startled by the ku-klux-klan of that gunlock, stopcock, and clockwork toing and froing associated with the streets of Manhattan in the bull days when young clerks, who called themselves bankers, first began walking to work wearing running shoes while carrying their walking shoes with them.

Secondly, it's the angle. In the streets of Italian cities, in Venice as in Florence or Rome, women move with a hyperbolic serenity, with that stochastic smoothness which flows naturally from the notion of an easily and pleasurably achieved moral aim. The overall impression is that of the graceful Brownian swarming one expects to find at the threshold of an Oriental gateway, whether what lies beyond the gate is a mere sultan's bedchamber or some heavenly paradise. I quote from the Second Sura of the Glorious Qur'an, which a Syrian girl called Hala once gave me for my birthday on the charming and solemn condition that I always keep it on the topmost shelf of my bookcase:

> To each is a goal
> To which he turns;
> Then strive together
> Towards all that is good.
> Wheresoever ye are,
> God will direct you.

This really is the philosophical layout of a typical piazza in an Italian town, a theatrical souk studded with busy cafes and encrusted with somnolent shops, where the chorus of women swirls through the ranks of seated, or at least contemplative, men like a jewelled comb through a storybook beauty's hair. God is a good director. His productions are interesting.

By contrast, even in the King's Road, Chelsea's perennial tourist seraglio with a reputation for charivari, incense and idleness surviving from another era, one rarely catches a glimpse of anything other than the abrupt zig of the angular shoulder and the nervous zag of the plastic mannequin head. My point is that, to men, women represent life, and I've grown tired of looking at life that is all jagged shards, as though in a smashed rearview mirror of a badly parked builder's van. I wonder if this means I've finally grown tired of London.

The fashionable cinema in the King's Road is showing a new American film called *Charlie's Angels*. Ordinarily, in the history of the imagination of the world, east or west, angels belong to God and are God's, but in Hollywood they are Charlie's. Accordingly, on the film's posters, the actresses chosen for the part of angels appear to be angular, scrawny, hostile, wingless and frozen in the abortive indelicacy of a martial arts pose. Please imagine a painting in which a divine messenger might be required to make an appearance, such as the Annunciation, and judge what sort of Virgin, and what kind of God, would be consistent with the face and the demeanour of one of these creatures. As though to complete the bestial conceit, the actresses have been photographed and celebrated in the press upon being presented to the Prince of Wales, heir to the throne and defender of the faith. *Charlie's* angels, get it?

The mass image is so radically and incontrovertibly a new departure in the history of the Eternal Feminine that an Italian magazine has produced a cover story on the emerging global trend masterminded by Hollywood towards *un fisico bestiale*, a bestial physique. The accompanying cry of dissent, an anguished counterclaim that "*a noi piacciono sempre morbide,*" we Italians still like them soft, is supported by a huge photo-still of the superstar of the moment – Monica Bellucci, *tutta curve* – all curves, now appearing in Giuseppe Tornatore's film *Malèna*, a story of seduction set in Sicily that has been setting box-office records. In the picture, Miss Bellucci is clad in the nostalgic and intricate armour of femininity that brings to mind the Raymond Chandler phrase "cute as lace pants."

It is interesting to note that all the places where women have cast off womanhood down to the last, seventh veil, such as the United States, Germany, Holland, and the Scandinavian countries, are famous for both the production and the proliferation of pornography. The places where women continue to exhibit the hyperbolic serenity of which I speak, such as France, Italy, and the rest of the Mediterranean countries verging on the Muslim world, are equally famous for the design and manufacture of women's clothes, including lace pants, which is a much bigger industry than pornography. In other words, no sooner does the woman publicly declare herself free to become a judge, a priest, or a banker than she is made to strip naked in public. Whereas in the absence of such a vociferous declaration, while in fact being perfectly free to judge, pray, or bank as she wishes, the woman is a protected object of veneration and a mainstay of the national economy.

I am neither flirting with Islamic fundamentalism, nor affecting the bar-room habits of thought now called male chauvinism, but merely doing what I have done since coming to Italy, that is, using the modern, changing London as a foil for my increasingly real life over here. My Venetian friend Andriana M— is in her seventies, but in the foggy aftermath of a supper I gave her she found no fewer than three telephone numbers inside her handbag, all slipped in there by rather younger men who were so taken by her beauty, her charm, and her wit that they had forgotten that three-quarters of a litre of vodka, even when chased down with pickled mushrooms, marinated herrings, and sturgeon caviar, divides into three with perilous consequences. My neighbour Donatella A— is only half a generation behind, yet so luminous is her face, so serene her movement, and so hypnotic her whole dynamic silhouette, that it is not uncommon for men of almost any age to freeze, open-mouthed, while watching her cross Campo S. Stefano in the company of a golden retriever. And Stella C—, a young mother, tragically widowed, vestal, with the face of a Cimabue Madonna, is somebody to whom I imagine an absolute stranger will one day propose, on bended knee, with a small bouquet of roadside daisies from the dusty mainland and a diamond rivière from Chatila in the middle of a crowded *vaporino* during the lunchtime rush hour.

Such are the human types whose fascination I can never see waning, and the streets of London now strike me – as the streets of Manhattan did twenty, and more than twenty, years ago – as almost completely bereft of the life they represent. They are the actresses who have been auditioned by God, the director, and chosen to play the part of the angels in an action film without an opening sequence, whose final meaning is civilization. They are now being blacklisted, pushed out, and replaced by Charlie's globally projected inventions, with the immediate prospect of barbarizing mankind more effectively than any religious fanaticism or political doctrine. For what all the artefacts of civilization – our basilicas and our railway stations, our iconic Madonnas and our reclining odalisques, our farthingales and our lace pants – ever had in common was that they made up a spectacle worth watching. Well, no more, says Hollywood. No more, repeats Madison Avenue. No more, echoes the King's Road.

This is why the women's movement is all wrong. *Un fisico bestiale* and a boring, boring director.

… un fisico bestiale and a boring, boring director

XXXIV Cortina d'Ampezzo

Roman Holiday

Once in a while, though not too often, one has the occasion to discover that deep down beneath the surface things are actually better than they seem. Some years ago, when she was unequivocally and irresponsibly young, my English friend Natasha G— came to stay with her godfather, Franco Zeffirelli, at his villa in Positano, where a newly famous Russian called Misha Baryshnikov was also a house guest. With her godfather's blessing *in loco parentis*, Misha took to inviting the teenage daughter of a peer of the realm to nightclubs and discotheques, and eventually fell madly in love with her. Recently I asked Natasha why she had broken so cruelly the uncommonly heterosexual heart of the Nijinsky of our epoch. "Well, you see," she remembered with a certain visible distaste, "he kept asking me out, and I just hated the way he danced. It was *really* embarrassing."

The moral of the story will arrive later today. Though I write this crouching behind a hotel room desk in Rome on what feels like a warm spring afternoon, with the Forum's white marble bones showing through the open window like the bleached skeleton of some unlamented casualty of social evolution, my mind keeps turning back to Cortina, with all that rude good health, sparkling with snow and brimming with mulled wine. I have just come back, after two weeks of pretending to ski alongside the Romans who make this Alpine village what it is, a wintertime watering hole for those apparently uncomplicated individuals who believe that social evolution is not something to worry about when one can drip with diamonds, swathe yourself in furs, and eat veal cutlets with fresh artichokes in the bar of the Hotel de la Poste instead. In short, modern Romans, not unlike their ancient ancestors who sold prize specimens of hog outside my hotel window, like to enjoy themselves. This they do in Cortina.

From the perspective of Venice, which is only an hour and a half away by car, Cortina belongs to Rome the way Aspen belongs to New York, the City of London belongs to Wall Street, and Art belongs to the Muses. Venetians see the place as a playground of the great Roman *cafone*, that is to say boor, bounder, lout, *arriviste* and cad, a cross between Shakespeare's Falstaff and a New Russian, with a chromosomal admixture of the Essex Man and a genetic pinch of the Bridge and Tunnel. "God, those clowns!" my friend Giovanni exclaims, with a smile bitter as wormwood. "You should watch them eat. How they eat! Like marathon swimmers, face to the right. *Ha-a-a-rgh!* Then face to the left. *Ha-a-a-rgh!* And then you see them *coming up for air.*" His portrayal is accurate, and in the already mentioned bar of the Poste one can still watch live the orgiastic scenes I remember witnessing in places like Al Moro, not far from the Quirinale, in the days before Rome began to persecute its crooks as hypocritically as it once persecuted its Christians.

Outside the habitat he has colonized, such as Cortina in winter and the Costa Smeralda in summer, the *cafone* sticks out like a sore thumb. A few months ago I went to the Palafenice – the

… who believe that social evolution is not something to worry about

temporary structure at Tronchetto meant to stand in for Venice's old Gran Teatro La Fenice until all the money for its reconstruction has been stolen – to hear Angela Brown in Verdi's *Requiem*:

> Libera me, Domine, de morte aeterna,
> in die illa tremenda,
> quando caeli movendi sunt et terra...

When the performance was over, and the audience started leaving the theatre, we saw that Venice had flooded. As though conjured up by the music, *acqua alta* had come in on cue, and getting home, at any rate without rubber boots up to your ears, was out of the question until the water receded. How long this would take, thirty minutes or three hours, was anyone's guess. Standing next to me in the crowd was a Roman couple, instantly recognizable by the Hermès orange of his scarf and the purple mink of her coat, who would surely have brought to any mind more socially restive than mine the lush English expression "pigs in clover." And the sow – I mean, the lady – was furious. "How long is this going to take?" she kept asking. As I say, nobody knew the answer. Finally, as her exasperation reached a climax, she shrieked with a fury surpassing the *Dies irae* we had just heard: "Somebody please call Rome!" As you or I might have shrieked, in slightly different circumstances, for the switchboard to put us through to the Lubyanka.

This, then, is the ugly side of holidaying in Cortina, at least from the Venetian point of view. But as the story of my princess and the frog she refused to dance with illustrates, the moral nexus between repulsive appearance and charming essence is knotted the Gordius way even in children's fairy tales. In real life one must try to dig ever deeper, and when I go to Cortina, as I have now done for about ten Christmases running, I go with the intention of watching the Romans do what they no longer can do in Rome, and of admiring them.

Consider the dynamics of social interaction – ideally, from the expensive vantage point of the open-air terrace of the Poste, dry martinis $15, olives included – between old acquaintances. These can really only be described with recourse to a furrier's specialist terminology, and I know that nobody is going to believe me, but if a fifty-year-old woman is wearing a three-quarters-length Canadian sable by Ferré, then the friend she happens to bump into on the terrace will be wearing a coat of the same fur and of the same length. So if it's chinchilla worked in asymmetrical swirls then chinchilla worked in asymmetrical swirls it's going to be, just have a drink, wait for a couple of minutes, pop a green olive in your mouth... Well, what d'I tell you? There's her friend, coming round the corner in white après-ski boots with CHANEL on them. Chinchilla! Asymmetrical swirls!

"*Ciao cara*, you always look wonderful in that." "Hello darling, and you in that." Come to think of it, the people here don't have friends, they have cheval-glass reflections. They don't have thoughts and conversations, they have furriers and jewellers. But now, just before the second martini, is the time to ask: Is that bad? Is it really better to conform to the global rule of "be yourself" and "be what you want to be," which of course has been promulgated in order to ensure maximum homogeneity the world over, a homogeneity of militant pseudo-individualism veiling all classes and conditions of men with a blue-denim pall, or is it better to rebel as the people in this alpine oasis do, to live like a *cafone* among the *cafoni*, to be with your own kind, to move in the company of your own ethical and aesthetic doubles, and feel no shame?

They shiver at the thought of wearing furs in Aspen. In New York, they buy fake pearls from Kenneth Lane. Hardly anybody in St. Tropez remembers how a dry martini is mixed. Does this make *their* social twins any less identical? Does it make their lives less predictable, more introspective, more subtle? Do we really suppose that the German woman in a nylon parka with a fake ocelot trim talking to her friend in jeans and a sheepskin vest about the political situation in the Middle East – and *not even once* addressing her as "darling" – is any less of a fake bitch, and would have any more interesting things to say, than the splendid Roman *cafona* now traversing the field of vision in front of my table? Waiter, I'll have another. I want to toast the magnificent conformity of this stubborn microcosm of yours.

And again I return to the story of my friend and her putative lover. Had the world's greatest dancer had but the smallest share of the rebellious stubbornness of these Romans in Cortina, he would have taken her to the ballet instead. Natasha Baryshnikova! Now, that has a ring to it. I think I shall send her a postcard.

XXXV Parma

Leningrading Verdi

Foreigners often think of life in Italy as operatic, which shows that reinvestment in the obvious is not always a losing proposition. If only more foreigners had followed Nietzsche in asking, "If it is true that evil men have no songs, how is it that the Russians have songs?" then perhaps the world would not have become the plaything of wickedness that it is today. And there you have it. All the themes I intend to touch upon in describing my visit to the Teatro Regio in Parma are more or less audible in my opening paragraph.

At the Regio, as part of the Verdi Festival's *Celebrazioni Nazionali* commemorating the centenary of the composer's death, Valery Gergiev led the *Orchestra Kirov del Teatro Mariinskij di San Pietroburgo* in a performance of *Un Ballo in Maschera*, with Ivan Momirov as Riccardo, Sergei Murzaev as Renato, and Olga Sergeeva as Amelia. *Regia: Andrej Konchalovskij.* The name of the person identified in the programme as *responsabile dei progetti speciali*, I was amused to note in the interval, was Kalashnikov.

I should enlarge on this symbolic coincidence by noting further that the Kirov is generally in a bit of trouble these days. They cannot really go on calling themselves the Kirov because names like the Goebbels Playhouse or the Pol Pot Skating Rink or the Amin Luncheonette are no longer in fashion. The fact that, as our parents used to sing,

> We's so upset and so worried-o,
> 'Cos Stalin bumped 'im off in a corridor,

does little to restore to the Kirov name some of its original Bolshevik dignity. Equally, they cannot change it back to the Imperial Mariinsky because in the West nobody will come, especially those commercially vital ballet audiences of provincial mothers who have been brought up on matinée idols like The Kirov's Own!! Rudolf Nureyev!!! In Moscow, the Bolshoi was luckier for the Bolsheviks. It looked as though they had shrewdly named themselves after the theatre.

Without dispute, Gergiev is one of the leading conductors of our day. But, as far as I am concerned, the real trouble he has to deal with is that during the seventy years of Soviet rule Russia did not produce even *one* singer worth hearing. Naturally, you may not say "Smirnov" or "Chaliapine" or "Figner" because that would be lying; they had been world famous by 1917, and mentioning them is like giving credit to the *New York Times Book Review* for having encouraged Emily Dickinson. And please, I beg you, don't say "Obraztsova" or "Vishnevskaya," or I'll turn around and walk away; we're talking Italy here, we're talking the Verdi season, we're talking the Teatro Regio di Parma. Here, in 1837, they actually *rejected* young Verdi. Here, in 1916, Amelita Galli-Curci sang Gilda.

... thought him perfectly charming

I have the recording, and I can only explain the cultural difference between a Galli-Curci and a Vishnevskaya as the distance between a painting by Ingres and a work of socialist realism, though of course one mustn't assume that this explanation will satisfy everybody. As it happened, on the way to Parma I stopped off in Bologna to see an exhibition of Soviet art at the Palazzo Re Enzo. "Could it be," the authors of the catalogue rhetorized, incredulously and indignantly, "that Stalin's regulations had swept away the artists' expressive capacities, and so filled their consciences as to transform them into mere illustrators of state propaganda?" I don't want to insult anybody, but a hall in the vaulted walkway beneath the Palazzo Re Enzo has a famous acoustic peculiarity, which a friend demonstrated to me after we had seen the exhibition. You talk to the wall, and it talks back. It's very Red Bologna, that.

Later that night in Parma we went out to dinner with the only Italian singer in the production, the almost indecently beautiful and almost indescribably gifted Laura Giordano, who sang Oscar. The extravagant compliment I paid her was almost entirely true, namely, that just because we Russians can write books better than the Americans and build better tanks than the Germans does not mean that we should carry *pelmeni* (ravioli, actually) to Parma, that is to say, to sing Verdi at the Teatro Regio. In fact, the tenor Ivan Momirov is Bulgarian, but since he had been audibly booed – in Milan he would have been whistled – I generously included him, too.

In the interests of fairness I must add that Konchalovsky's staging made for a most beautiful production – in the last scene the curtain parted with a fireworks of glittering baubles that seemed to have been disgorged by the magnificent ballroom itself, like a Fabergé ornament being given birth by a Versace hetaera in a painting by Galanin – but then again I never did say that our boys couldn't do theatre, or play a musical instrument, or even paint as well as the next KGB man. And yet, mysteriously, they've never been able to sing grand opera, and so after our dinner with *la Laura* I decided to proceed to another restaurant in town, where the Russians were celebrating, to learn where Gergiev had found the chutzpah (*palle*, actually) to carry coals to Donbass. I had met the conductor once before, in London, at a dinner given by Donatella Flick at her house in Hyde Park Gate, and thought him perfectly charming, as the mothers who did not want me to date their daughters used to say about me, their lips tightening with menace. "Yes, he is charming. *Charming.*"

But now I must cast off the harmless misdeeds of my remotest past for the sake of one fairly crucial observation. Opera is important to Italy because only in opera does the Italian language become *national* in any meaningful sense; and, as if that were not important enough, only in opera does that language become *international*, in the sense in which French is often acknowledged as the language of diplomacy, or English the language of science. Singing Italian opera is every note a linguistic exercise, and listening to a fellow who knows no Italian singing Verdi is like seeing a professor of Russian literature at the University of California barging into a Chekhov play in a nylon tracksuit.

It is as though the architectonic structure of musical sound translates itself into the living and breathing chimera of native Italian speech, just as a competent architect can render a building by means of a technical drawing; whereas a foreigner's accent imperceptibly erodes and eventually undermines the entire musical structure. The travesty is all the more dastardly for being virtually undetectable, rather the way somebody out of his head on cocaine may appear perfectly normal to his own children. Russian grammatical forms, in particular, often mimic the Italian (*andate* is *idite*), while shared etymologies ensure that *occhi* do not look all that different from *ochi* in a dimly lit libretto. Thus I challenge any Henry Higginses out there to guess that a Russian singer stinks to high heaven on the basis of his elocution alone. Because, as here at midnight, when Amelia goes to gather her magic herbs in the graveyard, elocution *is* the music:

> Mezzanotte!.. ah! che veggio? Una testa
> Di sotterra si leva… e sospira!
> Ha negli occhi il baleno dell'ira
> E m'ffisa e terribile sta!

Once I had arrived at the restaurant where the Mariinsky braves were carousing, however, all was revealed. Amid the discordant cries of *"come si chiama*, rebyata, *questa cosa?"* and *"per favore*, devushka, *per favore!"* some thirty of my compatriots were busy commingling vodka with grappa, and there I stayed with them until six in the morning. No, none of them had any knowledge of the language beyond that of a prisoner in an internment camp, and when I finally managed to ask the lead baritone's wife, herself a respected soloist with the Bolshoi, how on earth they managed to sing in Italian, the sweet woman replied that since times immemorial Russian singers learned the words of the libretti by rote, often after first writing them out in Cyrillic characters.

By times immemorial she meant the year 1917.

XXXVI Venice

Up With Prejudice

I have been a Eurocentric, heterosexual, white male ever since I was a little baby. An unreconstructed Marxist would say that this accident of birth – carelessly amplified of late by the sybaritic sojourn in a palazzo on the Grand Canal whose windows watch the West decline over the campanile of Santa Maria Gloriosa dei Frari – is what has determined my consciousness for the remainder of my natural life, and of course the sonofabitch would be right. The thing about Marxism I have always thought unnerving is its directness, so reminiscent of New York dinner parties and conversations with one's wife's relatives. Show me your bank statements, says Che Guevara between puffs on a Cuba stout, and I shall tell you what sort of verses you scribble.

Hence those who know me may find it difficult to believe that a couple of weeks ago I decided to join a friend of mine travelling to Bombay. I had no special reason for going, except that I was curious. In fact, ever since I began learning English as a child in Moscow – by the thrilling, though labourious, process of tracing the etymology of each new word down to its Sanskrit root and finding the semantic node where one golden bough of our tree of languages divided from another – I had some peculiar fondness for ancient India, which neither Kipling nor Indian singing movies did anything to suborn. Thus I could read for hours on end about the worship of the Yoginis as the sixty-four manifestations of the great goddess Devi, yet what mattered to me was not the validity of the underlying belief, nor any of the incomprehensible speculations about the feminine creative force and the occult powers of the Puranic *matri*, but the fact that the chess queen of Russian fairy tales, Baba Yaga, was probably one of that brood.

We boarded the plane in England, where the nation's agriculture, already paralysed by one cattle plague, was now in the grip of another: MASS CULL ON FARMS WIDENS AS MARKSMEN ARE CALLED IN was among the banners headlining the apocalypse. Writing about India, Kipling put it like this:

> Look westward – bears the blue no brown cloud-bank?
> > Nay, it is written – wherefore should we fly?
> On our own field and by our cattle's flank
> > Lie down, lie down to die!

Parliament had recently voted by a vast majority to outlaw fox hunting, and the day's other news was that a band of animal rights protesters, wearing balaclavas and carrying "baseball bats and pickaxe handles," had attacked a 62-year-old angler on the banks of the Granta with shouts of "How many fish did you kill today?" and "How would you like a hook through your mouth?" Meanwhile, the Glasgow branch of a national chain of music shops had put on sale promotional shirts emblazoned with the slogan JESUS IS A C—, whereupon the Lord Provost of that city, staking his all on the reality of a Europe that no longer exists outside the places where I live, directed the police to have them removed.

"We pride ourselves on offering the largest range of products available," objected the shop's manager as he ordered the shirts restocked, "and leaving it to the customers to choose whether they wish to purchase them." As for me, I thought, I rather pride myself on being unable to repeat the obscenity in question even in a private conversation about the incident. I am a Eurocentric, heterosexual, white male, and consequently, for me, there are inhibitions which are infinitely more sacred than many a truth. It was in this state of mind, rubbed raw by the Sunday newspapers until it filled itself to the point of screaming with the pus of every ethical calamity I had witnessed while living in England, that I got off the plane and saw Bombay.

It too offered *the largest range of products available*, a promise which I ever suspected to mean at best a dirty towel but most likely a shallow grave. Despite the lateness of the hour and all our meek demurrers, the man behind the wheel of the hotel car who identified himself as "Driver Ghana, Car No. 1733" immediately conveyed us to a brothel. This brought to mind a television commercial of the Cold War epoch in which the same elephantine, and plausibly East European, presence paraded on the catwalk over and over again wearing the same shabby clothes, until the grand finale was announced ("And finally… beachwear!") when she appeared wearing them yet again, but this time cradling a beach ball in her enormous dimpled arms. In short, perhaps because the props were even thinner on the ground than the taboos, it was clear to me at once that love in Bombay was impossible.

What of life? The following morning the sun rose, laboriously, over the city and hung there, in the white sulphur mist, like the yolk of a rotten egg. It illuminated a hepatotoxic sea the colour of overripe bananas, and a seafront promenade filled with the cries of hundreds of young, healthy men selling recreational drugs and children's balloons: "*Balam, balam, balam, balam*! Hello? *Balam, balam, balam, balam*! Hello?" Nobody bought either, which only increased the sensation of having been awakened to a psychedelic rendition of some unknown canto of Dante's *Inferno*, the one about the Circle of Inflated Balloon Sellers, the adults condemned to hawk children's toys in a city where the children are busy panhandling.

Ah, those infamous children of India! Crippled, mutilated, filthy, with handsome, often refined, always serious faces, the children of India are busy begging alms from the tourists who come there, as a week's close observation of my hotel companions made me realize, for no purpose whatever other than *to feel white*, obviously a long forbidden pleasure in their countries of origin. The tourist industry's marketing of Asia and Africa is undoubtedly the most ruthless colonial exercise in the history of mankind, compared to which the pith helmets of the Raj and the bayonets of the Boers are so much incongruous balloon selling. If you want to find racism on a global scale, visit your local travel agent. He will tell you that if you really want to have fun you should go where dark people live on two cents a day.

Now, I have seen something of poverty. I was born in an apartment where thirty-five people, from nine families, lived under one leaky roof, sharing a bath and a telephone. But I tell you that

Bombay does not suffer from poverty, it suffers from bestiality. If you are a Russian living under Brezhnev on two roubles a day, as often as not you will find a bucket of paint to make your corner of a hopeless universe slightly more habitable; if you are an Italian living in the post-war slums of Naples on your mother's cooking, as often as not you will procure two metres of polka-dot georgette to make a blouse for Sophia Loren; but if you are an Indian living in Bombay under the shadow of a Coca Cola hoarding, you will do nothing but gaze, attentively yet dispassionately, upon a dusty road mined with rabid dogs, listening to the honking of horns in tin cars and munching on a chance scrap of venomous offal.

I fear that modern India is not only the immemorial past of Europe but its impending future. There was a time when we, too, worshipped the Yoginis, and hurricanes, and flowers, in the distant millennia before our civilization became centred on man, on God, and on its own destiny, yet judging by what I now glimpse in the Sunday newspapers, that time is fast upon us once more. For to defend a fish in the Granta from a barbed hook, and to save a fox in Hampshire from being hunted with hounds, is not only not merciful, kind, or Christian, it is an act of pagan sacrilege on a par with the blasphemy of the greedy shopkeeper of Glasgow; because to elevate beast to the place of man is to denigrate man to the level of beast.

The rivers in England, incidentally, are already the colour of overripe bananas. Unless the taboos of our civilization are held sacred – and those who offer us *the largest range of products available* are strung up on lamp-posts as a matter of course – the day will surely come when the descendants of those same Members of Parliament who now cast votes for human rights and animal progress will sit half-naked in Trafalgar Square, amid dysenteric refuse and choleraic waste, with the mongrel descendants of their neighbours' ancestral hounds for company. I cannot say that I am feeling unrelievedly tearful at the prospect.

... not only the immemorial past of Europe but its impending future

XXXVII Palermo

In the Mafia

A friend of mine just got arrested for arms dealing. From whom he was buying the arms, to whom he was selling them, or indeed whether he ever bought or sold any, I haven't the slightest idea. But the raid, by the Italian police and intelligence, on Sasha Zhukov's $5 million villa in Piccolo Romazzino, on Sardinia's Costa Smeralda, made front page news in London and in the Italian papers. It was in London, in fact, that we had first met, and a year later Sasha came out to a dinner party in Venice in the company of his fiancée, a glamorous former Miss Greece. Too thin for my taste, mind you, but then again, with the Greeks, time is on your side.

We were introduced by a mutual friend called Galya, whose estranged husband, the Russian entrepreneur Boris Berezovsky, keeps an apartment in the same fortified enclave of London's "embassy row" where Sasha bought himself a penthouse overlooking Kensington Palace. By way of a brief digression the reader may as well hear what in Heaven's name the vituperative Doubting Thomas and bilious helpmate of White Counter-Revolution, the so-called writer and self-styled freethinker Navrozov, is doing running around with people of that peculiar stripe. Would Luis Farrakhan choose to dine with *his* natural enemies? Would Norman Podhoretz pay for *your* dinner? Is there no such thing as principle?

The answer is that when, in the early 1980s, Andropov's secret-police apparatus relaunched Beria's old plan for the restructuring of Soviet totalitarianism – to be marketed at home and abroad as the fall of communism – Russia's ruling junta needed a human face for their emerging system. Like an Identikit portrait, this was to be made up of a few predictable elements, including free elections to a legislative body without power, independent media with a material base controlled by the state, and unlimited business opportunities for those chosen to enjoy them. Not much in the way of verisimilitude, but if you are the chief executive officer of a multinational corporation itching to sell your country down the river, it's more than enough to bring round your stodgiest shareholder.

Anyway, punters like Berezovsky and Zhukov were among the lucky ones. I'm not saying that they had got a head start by keeping their distance from the secret police, or that they had been picked to play the part of entrepreneurs in the pantomime of Russian capitalism just because they had a firm handshake and an engaging smile. But by the time auditions were held, the specific loyalties of the men who were going to make up what would soon become popularly known as the Russian mafia hardly mattered. The premise was that a certain percentage of the country's wealth, say 5%, would be turned over to them – as had been done once before during the New Economic Policy of the 1920s – and their inborn greed, human vanity, and a modicum of effort would do the rest. In a matter of a few years, the simulacrum of capitalism in Russia would have a pockmarked but convincingly human face. As for controlling this mafia, since when does a 95% stakeholder worry about how to control the small fry?

… picked the right numbers and received their reward from the hand of fate

So much for the digression, the point of which is that people like Sasha Zhukov are basically good fellows, living high on the hog, and endowed with a mentality very much like the lottery winner's. The only problem is that, like many lottery winners, they tend to reassess their lives *ex post facto*, reorganizing everything from kindergarten onwards into a logical chain of causes and effects that lead inexorably to the moment when they picked the right numbers and received their reward from the hand of fate. In never occurs to them that they are mere extras, expendable and replaceable, in a political production the likes of which the West has never dreamed possible. How could it ever occur to them? They take the West, with its Kensington penthouses and its Misses Greece, very seriously. So when they get taxed in Moscow, or shot in Cannes, or arrested in Piccolo Romazzino, they are very surprised.

The news of Sasha's arrest reached me at the Grand Hotel delle Palme in Palermo, where I have since decided to spend the coming summer. I had never visited Sicily before, and had it not been for the unexpectedly and fortuitously acquired friendship of the G—, a family of hereditary *Palermitani*, I would never have made the effort of tearing myself away from Venice at a time when the crab season was just beginning. Besides, like the Red Army of old, I only go where I am invited.

Alfredo G— brought me the day's *Corriere della Sera* with a happy smile on his face: "Friend of yours?" On seeing Zhukov's photograph next to the grim headline, I told him that I would normally regard the poor rich sucker as a passing acquaintance, but now that he was behind bars, and rather more probably put there by the hubris which is the nemesis of the lucky than by any real malfeasance, yes, I was more than happy to regard him as a friend. Afredo signalled his approval of my reasoning with a Masonic wink and, standing in a Palermo street and craning our necks like two *Superenolotto* savants scrutinizing the village by village distribution of the weekly jackpot, together we read the article.

The Milanese take on the news did not contain any references to arms smuggling, international intrigue, Russia, or the Balkans. The crux of the story was that in August of last year Sasha gave a party for 600 guests at his Sardinian love nest, where his immediate neighbours include Italy's George Bush, Silvio Berlusconi. Present among the celebrities were Alba Parietti (in American terms, roughly speaking, Martin Peretz coaxed into the body of Vanna White), Prince Carlo Giovannelli (Taki Theodoracopulos minus the wit, I regret to say, as well as the charm and the money), Marco De Benedetti with his wife Paola Ferrari (Sonny & Cher, if Sonny made $3 billion selling mobile phones), Robero Cavalli (no truly fêted Italian fashion figure has had an Anglo-American counterpart since Halston choked on ultrasuede), and so on down the length of the Roman social edifice, which was decorated for the occasion with a number of "girls with crystal tattoos sent over by an escort agency in Milan" and topped with a vase "containing twenty-two kilos of Beluga caviar."

"I already told the television people I don't know anything about him," said one grandee, Ignazio La Russa, "so what do you want me to say? This story shouldn't be making the papers." "I don't really know who Signor Zhukov is," said another guest, Paolo Cirino Pomicino, "but why should I feel embarrassed? I was just there by chance. I came with friends. I was staying with Daniela Santanchè… You know how she is, I always go where she tells me." In her turn, Daniela

Santanchè told the *Corriere*: "No, we had no idea who the Russian was. You know how it is in the summer here, it's like a caravan, one group just follows another. We dropped by only for a few minutes." Supposed to have crowed thrice in the story, the cock of the Gospels was by now more like a galvanically oscillating dead frog.

"You see? That's your Venetians for you," muttered Alfredo. I tried to explain that the perfidious gobblers of free caviar were Roman, Milanese, Bolognese, anything but Venetian, that Venice was less responsible, from the strictly ethnographic point of view, for the complexion of Italy's *beau monde* than just about any other Italian city you could mention. All was to no avail, because to Alfredo the distinction between any two places on the mainland, even as utterly dissimilar to the mainland dweller's mind as Milan and Venice, was dwarfed by their basic northernness, their cold and calculating northern baseness. If I had come from Florence, Alfredo would have said that leaving friends in a lurch was a Florentine trait. "They are all alike," he said. "*That* mafia. Not a grain of loyalty."

As for Palermo, I will have to wait and see.

XXXVIII Palermo

Untitled

Asked in ever more incredulous tones, the question is warm with sympathy on the lips of friends and cold as Damask steel in the mouths of enemies. "Why Palermo?" One frivolous reply is that, back in Venice, the crab season is now over; the white-sneaker hydra of package tourism is about to hot-millipede it over the bridges; and our cook, having just won $3000 after translating her dream of a school of fish into lottery numbers, has gone on holiday. Another is that our prospective apartment in S. Stae, which had been found at the eleventh hour just as the proprietor at Palazzo Mocenigo was threatening to call in the law, has a sitting tenant who will not leave before autumn. He is Paolo Costa, and I can't very well call in the law to throw *him* out because he is the Mayor of Venice.

Still another explanation is that once every two years, in high summer, my beloved Venice loses face and becomes a kind of cultural sewer. This is the season of the Biennale, the witches' Sabbath that brings all the world's scum to our canals by way of the art galleries, the charitable foundations, and for all I know the real-estate agencies and the massage parlours, of New York and London. I was there for the opening dinner, held on a converted tugboat belonging to the director of the Guggenheim, and was so repulsed by what I saw – not that I am easily repulsed, mind, least of all by massage parlours – that I took the next flight to London, figuring that everybody I loathe there was already busy networking in Venice. Fate was swift to reward me for my good judgement with a new insight.

Some months ago, at the country house of a mutual friend in England, I had met a young painter by the name of Sophie de S—, and now as soon as I arrived in London it transpired that she wanted me and my gambling friend Gusov to sit for a double portrait. We are still unsure about the title. *Two Losers? Last Bets? Russian Roulette? Neighbours by a Hundred?* But anyway, the idea is clear. Sophie, who has been painting since she was seventeen, began her life in art as a model for Lucian Freud, an inveterate gambler, and was well acquainted with Francis Bacon, whose profligacy at the tables was equally legendary. For us, it was the once-in-a-lifetime chance to be immortalized, in attitudes so long cherished, by someone who *understood*. Hence Gusov, who cannot stay still for a minute unless he is playing (we once sat side by side in the gaming room of Aspinalls for fourteen hours without eating, drinking, or using the toilet), turned up as scheduled at Sophie's studio, his picturesque hair dutifully on end.

The studio itself, where the painter sleeps, wakes, and works from dawn to dusk, can be described as a kind of modern art installation entitled *Insult to Modernism*, or *Far from the Venice Biennale*. The floor is a recrudescence of paint that brings to mind the term *impasto*, and every surface of the attic rooms bears witness to the daily, exhausting, and deeply physical struggle

...entertain the last painter in Europe with some rough tales from Palermo

between pigment and temperament. My conversation with Sophie began when I threw a cigarette butt on her floor and she, with the polite sarcasm of a croupier asked to accept a bet after the ball had dropped, said that her floor was not dirty, it was just covered in paint.

"Painting in art schools is more or less out now," writes the English critic Matthew Collings in his intentionally irreverent, and often unintentionally revealing, encyclopaedia of contemporary art. "You could easily go through your art school years today without doing one. But it's not true that you would actually be encouraged to never do one, or punished if you secretly did one." Every hour that Gusov and I sat for Sophie I had the growing sense that the severe silhouette of the inside of that bent elbow, just below the roll of the work-shirt sleeve, set in a luminous outline against the window frame, the sprawling black tree branches, and the streaming dark clouds of a foul London afternoon, belonged to the spiritual musculature of the last painter on earth. Remember the Last Man in Europe, Orwell's original title of *Nineteen Eighty-Four*? Well, in *that* ultimate, desperate sense.

She let me look at some of her family papers, kept in what I remember as a paint-splattered biscuit tin, or maybe it was a paint-splattered velvet box. Baron de S—, her grandfather, fled Russia after 1917, and as the connection established itself in the snaking copperplate of Winter Palace invitations and the old orthography of yellowed deeds and long-broken covenants, my already seething brain grew all the more inflamed. She was the Last Artist in Europe, and of course I was desperately curious to know what she thought of the mafia of her contemporaries, most of whom I had left behind in Venice the week before. Her hesitant replies reminded me of my first meeting with the English poet Charles Causley, when, as an angry young contributor to the various books pages, I had tried to goad him into agreeing with the thousand nasty things I had to say, in print and in private, about the literary figures then regnant. Well, Causley kept saying, you know, it's difficult, writing…

But now, as my eloquent loathing and my stammering fury broke in their turn on the granite detachment of Sophie's mildest ellipses, slowly I began to catch on to what it was that I always believed was so banal, and so evil, about contemporary artists. One day, after leaving her studio, I bought a copy of the Collings encyclopaedia, entitled *Blimey!*, and was gratified to find that my recent intuition was wholly supported by fact. Blimey indeed, I said to myself, because the truth is so simple. What is banal and evil about contemporary artists is that *they don't paint*. Just as contemporary architects don't build buildings, contemporary musicians don't play instruments, contemporary generals don't win wars, contemporary lawyers don't defend the innocent, and contemporary doctors don't kill their patients only because contemporary lawyers would take them to the contemporary cleaners if they did:

> Art wasn't about being in a studio creating. It was about being in a studio creating and then being in a smart white gallery and having a catalogue and reviews in art magazines and flying to different international art spots and having curators and professional uptight zombies of the artworld suck up to you briefly.

Perhaps Causley was not entirely justified in his quietist, elastic, almost Oriental, forbearance with respect to the monsters I was hoping to slay with my pen, but the fact remains that the writers whom I took turns describing as banal and evil were at least *writing books*. Here, by contrast, it is as though some wicked and slothful gardener raised on Thoreau – whom Western civilization, like a dowager empress breathing her dying wish, has at last permitted to let a thousand flowers bloom – has gleefully turned, instead of rakes, trellises, and seedlings, to the stack of penny dreadfuls in the potting shed. The analogy is not haphazard, because the Walden which the artists in question have been exploiting, ever since the moustache was stuck on the Mona Lisa, is literature. In short, their mafia is actually on my turf, and for this I have all the more reason to hate them.

Literature enters the picture with the title. That Francis Bacon, for instance, is to my mind among the finest painters the world has ever produced is neither here nor there; what is objectively true is that he *painted*, and every existing photograph of the interior of his studio bears witness to the fact that he painted *often*; so it is par for the course that the work which eventually won him recognition was entitled *Three Studies for Figures at the Base of a Crucifixion* (1945). Now, where is the literature in that? Conversely, it hardly matters that in my view an art mafioso like Damien Hirst has the soul of a crooked accountant trapped in the heart of a talentless clown; what is objectively true is that he never spent any time painting, and hence it is not surprising that the work which made him famous, a tank of formaldehyde containing a shark, was entitled *The Physical Impossibility of Death in the Mind of Someone Living* (1991).

The shameless separation of modern art from painting, drawing, and sculpture, and their concomitant substitution with literature, philosophy, and politics, have produced a kind of Hollywood of artistic expression, where the intellectual clichés of the past hundred years are collected, regurgitated, produced, directed, acted, made into pictures, and launched globally. Like Hollywood, this cinema of banal ideas is entirely in the hands of a ruthless mafia, concerned solely with the perpetuation of its prestige and the augmentation of its influence. Hence an artist like Sophie, with bills to pay for her turpentine and her chrome yellow, is as alien to the whole business as Chekhov would be to Paramount.

So perhaps we had better not think of the attic in Ladbroke Grove as an art installation entitled *Far from the Venice Biennale*. And perhaps Gusov and I should back off, and stop pestering Sophie about giving our portrait a provocative, entertaining, literary title like *Russian Roulette*. And next time I sit for her, if there is a next time, perhaps I should entertain the last painter in Europe with some rough tales from Palermo, instead of explaining to her how the mafia works in her home town.

XXXIX Palermo

Public Relations

"All the cars you see around here," yet another taxi driver bringing me from the Grand Hotel Villa Igiea to the congested centre of town began in a confidential undertone, "it wasn't always like that, you know. Before, it was all carriages." Then, after a pause that he reckoned was long enough for the average tourist to appreciate fully the historic significance of the news he had just imparted: "Would you like me to take you to the airport when you're leaving?" Well, I had news for him, and the news was that I wasn't leaving.

Coming from Venice to Palermo as something other than a tourist is a bizarre experience, a little like what I imagine a *Social Register* Brahmin might feel on having to move from the Park Avenue apartment he finally inherited from his great uncle to the most socially desirable building in Cincinnati. "Oooh," says practically everyone in Cincinnati, "have you seen where Mr. Brahmin is living? That amazing new place behind the shopping mall? And you can see the park from every window? He must've paid a million dollars for that." I don't want to offend anyone, because of course I've never been to Cincinnati and don't know if it has parks and shopping malls, but the point I'm making is actually not uncomplimentary. I can even believe that Cincinnati is a wonderful place to live. It's just that it probably wouldn't be as wonderful as the Upper East Side, in that New Yorker's considered opinion. And if he's got a wife, forget it.

All this is bolstered by the defensiveness of the average native, who wants to show the visitor from abroad all the things that, to his counterintuitive mind, make Palermo a social and cultural peer of Venice, Rome, or London. History? Before there were houses, we used to live in *huts*. Frescoed ceilings? There is a building around the corner from where my cousin lives, it's got those. Real pretty, *Ottocento*. Too bad they had to make it into a gas station after the war. Culture? We've got the university somewhere over there, I think. Or the *library*, anyway. No, that's the county court. Social life? There's now even a shop open on the Corso that sells *Chanelle!* You know, the French one. And so on, when what the fellow should be pointing out instead is that the octopus here is fatter, the girls are prettier, the coffee in every bar is better than the best outside of Naples, the pastries are the couture equivalent of what one finds elsewhere in Italy, and the Teatro Massimo is without exaggeration a world-class opera theatre.

The other nearly insuperable problem the *Palermitani* are up against is that in most tourist imaginations – those postcard places where Venice is sinking, Parisian cooking is all butter, English boys are molested nightly, and Santa Claus lives in the Kremlin – Palermo means the mafia. But, as I have more or less hinted on previous occasions, the rest of the world is sinking much faster than Venice in every conceivable sense; and just about every nation, every city, every social class, and every profession in this not yet completely totalitarian universe of ours boasts a mafia of one

…last week a little girl was kidnapped in the province of Trapani

sort or another. Some of these, like the lawyers in the United States, are so obviously powerful that they have no need of violence; others, like the internationale of contemporary art with its associated galleries, museums, and media, are so well entrenched that their pre-eminence is never questioned; while still others, like the Sicilian mafia or the *Propriétaires-Editeurs* of the Michelin Guide, are contented to perform their traditional roles in society, such as teaching people good manners and where to eat well.

"*Even in Palermo* we have the mafia," beamed the maitre d'hôtel at the famous Charleston in the resort suburb of Mondello, imperiously waving away my healthy and otherwise perfectly attractive packet of cash the other night as soon as Alfredo G— had winked that he was paying for dinner. One can say that this kind of joke would slip easily from the lips of any quick-thinking flunkey anywhere, but I would argue that here it has a more transcendent meaning. Social order before everything. *La cosa nostra* is good manners.

Last week a little girl was kidnapped in the province of Trapani. But apparently the brigands had picked on the wrong baby – a baby, as it were, with the right connections – because twenty-four hours later she was restored to her family, her clothes all new and with a tiny gold chain around her neck as an added sign of contrition. None the less, that same evening the child's grandfather went on the local television news to apologize to all of Sicily, saying that if he had offended anyone the slight had been inadvertent, and that in future he would take care to treat everybody better. I don't think I have ever seen a more elegant exercise in conflict resolution under any political system.

"And therefore?" you may interject. Well, I generally tend to put my money where my mouth is, and just at the moment my mouth is full of *cassata*, the nonpareil ricotta fruitcake of Sicily. Therefore I'm going to buy a summer place here, a decision as irrevocable as it is closely reasoned. I have now spent a month at Villa Igiea, the sister hotel of the Grand Hotel delle Palme, going around with Alfredo and his many friends, one of whom, Maglio O—, is a former mayor of Palermo and an incorruptible regionalist who has done time for not ever having joined the national political mafia, a crime which the politicians in Rome call *corruption*. ("Soon they'll be putting you guys in jail for not having been to Brussels," I jostled him, "and then you'll remember fondly the good old days, when all you had to do to get along was buy lunch behind the Quirinale for a couple of gluttons.")

My conclusion is that, like Venice, Palermo is capable of retarding social progress, and is hence a desirable place to live. But while in Venice social order, good manners, and unadulterated food are guaranteed by the unwritten constitution of that independent republic – by its morbidly inward-looking aristocracy, by its fantastically antiquated and intricate guild system, by its topographic insularity and historical peculiarities – here in Palermo the same result is all *fai da te*, with the mafia as the do-it-yourself underwriter of traditions, morals, manners, and social attitudes. In Venice, an African immigrant would be unlikely to pursue a local woman because just getting into a taxi to follow her boat would set him back about $100. In Palermo, he would be unlikely to pursue her because the first guy who did had his private parts cut off and exhibited on a lamp-post in his neighbourhood, with an explanatory note attached.

Ever careful not to mix genres, I have tended to avoid meeting any of the local grandees, members of the fabled Sicilian aristocracy to whom many in Venice, in particular, are related by marriage. They have more or less abandoned Palermo, their great houses now crumbling tenements occupied by legal and illegal squatters, and it is quite clear that their names and escutcheons count for nothing in a place that has had to survive without them for so many generations. The power here – the power to resist progress, I mean, that being the only species of power I am interested in at this late stage of my intellectual development – is entirely in the hands of the native Palermitan middle class with the right connections. As far as I have seen, they are using that power to good effect, feathering their nests and dowering their daughters instead of building universities and opening art galleries.

Consider the result, which hardly recommends the magical place that everybody around here seems to think I come from. Even though I intend to live and hope to die in Venice, it has taken me fourteen months of anguished social climbing to find an apartment to rent on the Grand Canal. I've had to wear masks of wealth, amiability, and crushed velvet; I've had to pretend that I was Marino Falier risen from the dead; I've had to gamble on reputations of friends and plead with presumed enemies. To find an apartment to buy in Palermo, an entire *piano nobile* staring down the most beautiful square in the city with its eight balconies – or maybe it was twelve, I can't remember now – took an afternoon. A local architect and his building team are already there, inside the long-abandoned *Ottocento* folly, ripping up the floor and putting in the requisite middle-class appurtenances of water boilers, air conditioners, and door handles. Naturally, we didn't just walk in there. You don't start feathering your nest in Palermo unless you're told you can. Social order before everything. We are *protected*, you see.

"Well, I sure as hell hope so," is all the sham Venetian actually manages to say, between mouthfuls of freshly made ricotta fruitcake.

XL Palermo

To Get Something Done

"Before I have my coffee I want a glass of lemon juice," I say to the barman. He is out of lemons, which apparently can happen even in Sicily. "Oranges?" Out of oranges, but I suppose this too can happen. "What can I get then?" He offers me a lemon *granita*, made with crushed ice and sugar, out of his freezer. "Too sweet?" He swears it isn't, setting before me a small champagne glass of what exudes the freshest and most definitive flavour of locally grown lemons I have ever experienced. Yet the fact remains that the concoction in question is meant to be a kind of dessert. It is much too sweet to put in your mouth first thing in the morning.

But, killingly sweet though it is, this one is undeniably the best of the genre, two Michelin crowns and worth a special detour. So what is there to say, in the circumstances? Anyway, I eat the whole lot in a hypnotic silence, whereupon, mistaking my qualified admiration for unconditional surrender, the righteous barman begins the morning lesson: "I don't make it too sweet. Other people make it too sweet, when they shouldn't. I never do, because I'm careful. You have to be careful with *granita*. Never too sweet. You want to know something? It's all a matter of how much sugar you put in. If you put in too much, it becomes too sweet. But if you don't put in enough, it may be too sour." Humbly I ask for a large glass of water.

What I sometimes miss, living here, is Aristotelian logic. In the Anglo-American system of cultural values, at least some small portion of the stuff seems to filter through, down to the commonest man, along such admittedly inefficient capillaries as high-school education and white-collar employment, with the result that when you ask a Manchester banker for a debt-consolidation loan and his bank doesn't give them, he won't offer you chocolate kisses, or a gaily decorated wastepaper basket, instead of the money. Nor, still more obviously, will a Philadelphia baker, sold out of the bread rolls you wanted, ply you with perfectly ripe figs from his garden. If it is churlish not to give credit where credit's due, then all those gruesome multiple-choice, intelligence-quotient, standard-aptitude riddles the Americans are brought up on, and trained to solve from kindergarten to grave, may well appear in a somewhat less sinister light.

By contrast, in Italy – and Sicily, mind you, is practically in North Africa – categorical ratiocination is like a faint echo of something that has rushed past without leaving a deep trace, all but muffled by the daily intercourse of life, tradition, and custom. Noisy, colourful, and centred on improvisation, rather like a Moroccan souk, Italian thought is based on the principle that so long as you start with an abundance of honest ingredients – good pistachios, sound grammar, local building materials, marital fidelity, ripe aubergines – it cannot possibly matter all that much where exactly you end up, because the result will be pleasing *lo stesso*, anyway. There is never a plan, a project, a concept, a recipe, because that ubiquitous "anyway" is nothing less than the fundamental,

... because the result will be pleasing *lo stesso*

collectively upheld law of existence, and stronger than any individual act of intellection. If Italy as a nation has a way, it is anyway.

And, as I say, nowhere more than here in the scorching hot south, where you can easily feel oppressed by the often-mindless rhyming doggerel of marzipan sweetmeats and oozing figs that you end up with, time and again, in place of the hard-edged prose of life you may actually have had in mind. Which is all very well, even if you have to mutter to yourself all the while that it is your own nitpicking brain that is actually at fault, that you must change, that you would do well to adapt and to forget, that none of it really matters, because soon enough you observe that the result is pleasing *lo stesso*, whereupon you relax and the whole cycle repeats itself from the beginning. Which is all very well, I repeat, except when you are actually – actually, yes, really and truly, absolutely seriously, cross my heart and hope to die, thank you very much and I don't want any sugared almonds! – trying to get something done. Like building a house, for example.

Or at least rebuilding one, which is what I'm trying to do at present. Partly cerebral, with a modicum of planning, designing, and reasoning, this task is producing the curious cinematic split-screen effect of persuading me that I'm surrounded by small children while convincing the children – who are being paid perfectly adult, or at least adolescent, sums of money for their participation in the charade – that I'm a child, prone to tantrums, yet easily mollified with sweets or a new rattle. The case on the left of the screen is not hard to make, because people who all talk at once, don't listen to anybody, love every kind of noise so long as it's really loud, never take notes or write anything down, prefer pocket knives to fountain pens, cannot remember to switch on their telephones, are always snacking and talking about their mothers, would be regarded as children anywhere except Italy. Thus if you ask an architect whether or not the antique bath he had stolen to order from an abandoned villa in Catania will fit in the guest bathroom, given that the bath is 170 cm. long, he will tell you how ingeniously the bath was stolen, what perils he had faced, how he intends to recondition it, and what his mother said when he told her he would be storing it in her dining room. The one thing the man will never do is measure the distance between the walls and subtract 170.

Unfortunately, the case on the right is just as compelling. The client who bargained for an ordinary bath is presented instead with a bath to end all baths, rampant on lion's feet and fit for an English marquess. Yet he seems unhappy. All right, so maybe it won't go into the guest bathroom, maybe it can be used in the master bathroom, or as a drinks cabinet, or as an end-table. Or maybe it can be cut in a certain way, turned upside down and affixed to the ceiling with Murano chandeliers inside it (there is a really nice pair, as it happens, in an abandoned town house not far from the police station), *sarebbe bellissimo, sai*, but anyhow, why is the client unhappy, whimpering like a baby? It's a beautiful thing, it will all work out in the end, because no matter how we go about the job, the final result will be pleasing anyway.

Today is the feast day of S. Rosalia, the patron saint of Palermo. I walk with the crowd, twenty or thirty thousand people following the eight-foot-high reliquary of delicately worked solid silver carried through the city, as it has been on this afternoon in July for the last three hundred years. Come nightfall there are fireworks, and octopus-shaped balloons, and stands selling melon slices, nuts, and candy. The crowd grows still more numerous, swelling with village folk, yet the ensuing merriment – without drugs, without drink, without loose women, without Disneyland, without anything, in short, that any adult outside of Italy would regard as fun, because only small children can appreciate pointless noise, and just milling about, and watermelon that smells like the sea – is as decorous as the Royal Enclosure at Ascot on Ladies' Day.

I am the client, and at this juncture I feel that I have to ask myself: Are they not right? Have these people not built enough cathedrals, painted enough frescos, designed enough gardens, carved enough marble, cast enough bronze, chased enough gold and silver, and reconditioned enough stupid baths on lion's feet, to know something the client doesn't? Why must he insist on vinegar when they bring him precious wines, and on stones when they give him soft white bread, and on plain lemon juice in place of that historic *granita*? Why doesn't he have enough faith – or perhaps credulity, which is yet another childly commodity they seem to have in such great abundance – in their civilization, founded though it is on what he perceives as afterthought, happenstance, and caprice? "Besides, you are a writer. Is not literature based on these very things? You are also a gambler. Can't you entertain the thought of playing roulette with water taps and door hinges? And is love, for instance, so much a matter of knowing how everything will turn out in the end? Shame on you!"

And so, yet again, the client resolves to be good. The whole thing will get done, somehow, and the ingeniously stolen bath will fit somewhere, I suppose, and the architect won't come down with chicken pox or get the colic, or end up in jail, or get run over by a car while chasing a ball in the middle of the street, and the accounts will reconcile, and a planning permission won't really be necessary after all, and the apartment will be beautiful, and we will all sit down like a bunch of Moroccan street urchins in the cosy kitchen, munching on candied fruit and drinking raisin-sweet wine from Pantelleria, and we will look back and say, dear God, that was a close one, that almost didn't work out, though in the end I guess it has anyway, *lo stesso*. What price Aristotelian logic, then?

XLI Panarea

Night and Day

The reader may remember that when I first clambered onto the Italian carousel, at Piazza della Fontana di Trevi, my impressions were a kind of paean to the seriousness of Roman life. Now, some four years later and roughly four hundred kilometres to the south, I find myself in Palermo marvelling at the unconstrained childishness of the people. I dare say that those who would seize upon this apparent contradiction, suggesting that the dreamer has finally come down to earth, have never been to a fairground and never bothered to observe children at play.

There are, after all, some children who are good, that is to say serious, although they are usually a beleaguered minority. They are the ones whose games are a pleasure to watch. Obviously this does not mean one can ask them to balance the cheque book or move the car, and at times they may seem somewhat boisterous, but on the whole they are an altogether different breed from the autistic, rowdy, collectivist animals that the term "jungle gym" – fusing, as the Protestant world often does, the untrammelled nature of J. J. Rousseau with the careful nurture of Hitler Youth – brings to mind. In fact, I would say that nice children are as unlike these gum-chewing automatons as St. Francis of Assisi is unlike Martin Luther, or as the Mediterranean is unlike the North Sea. So if the Italians are at all like children, then my argument is that they are like *nice* children.

The island of Panarea, where I spent a couple of weeks honing that point to satisfaction, is one of the half-dozen small volcanic islands that lie off the northern coast of Sicily. Unlike its equally beautiful Aeolian neighbours, Stromboli, Salina, Lipari, Alicudi, Filicudi, and Vulcano, which are mostly visited by families from Naples and Palermo during the summer holidays – cue the 1950s, old issues of *Life* stacked up in the whitewashed boathouse, and the canoe scene from *The Seven-Year Itch* – Panarea of late has been making the society pages of glossy magazines in Milan, Paris, and London. The reason is Raya, and Raya is *un night pieno di vip*.

Before this charming and, in Anglo-American social terms, hopelessly misleading formulation can be interpreted, I ask the reader to follow me to a very different playground, whose nightlife I had the opportunity to observe earlier in the summer. Ibiza, where some English friends of mine just bought a house in the hills, is of course only nominally part of Catholic Spain, its summer population almost entirely made up of nightclub revellers from Britain, Germany, Holland, and the Scandinavian countries, with a sprinkling of Americans to lend authenticity to the enterprise. This is because much of the music played in the island's clubs by celebrity disc jockeys is American, in the sense that all the amplified noise, a prerecorded combination of words and sounds, is produced and packaged in the United States.

I thought I had some inkling of what that meant, recalling successfully a popular song from the late 1970s entitled *Ring My Bell*. In retrospect I'm proud to remember the name of the diva, Anita Ward, whose offering astonished me at the time by its Sapphic simplicity. But in Ibiza I

… my argument is that they are like *nice* children

realized that, as a composer, compared to the American music now going, Miss Ward was Mahler, if not Schoenberg. As a poet, she was difficult, almost obscure. I'm no musician, but the lyric content of what I heard in Ibiza was along these lines:

> Piece… of… meat.
> Piece… of… meat.
> Piece… of… meat.

Even after a quarter of an hour, or roughly five minutes to make out each word, I could still have been wrong, of course. It might have been fuzzy feet, or ear of wheat, or peace to Crete, or something about the heat.

Eight of us ended up in the "VIP section" of a nightclub called Pacha, leaving behind $2000. Commercially speaking, these establishments are extremely conventional catharsis machines which operate exactly like the strip joints of old Soho, where a Japanese tourist in London might go attracted by the false advertising of all manner of debauchery over the front door, only to be robbed of his cash and credit cards and thrown out the back into an even smellier alley. Culturally speaking, however, they are a thing to see, because while the elevated "VIP section" was still empty at 5 AM, obviously as symbolic as the cake to which young debutantes used to curtsy in the absence of royalty, the dance floor below was the dialectical synthesis of the "individual conscience" of Luther and the "proletarian masses" of Marx. Of course I always knew they were one and the same, these two Kraut bugaboos, but it isn't often that one actually gets to stare into the dilated pupils of one's political intuition.

The spectacle I was witnessing had little to do with drugs, despite Ibiza's reputation as the drugs capital of Europe. It had little to do with morality and immorality, with sex and rock 'n' roll. What lay before me on the dance floor below, stretching as far as the eye could see, had come straight from the archival footage of Nuremberg. "Piece of meat," roared the state-of-the-art speaker, and five thousand bodies jerked as one in reply. As at Nuremberg, it did not really matter what the lyric content was, and whether the larger-than-life speaker was denouncing the Jews who would take away our meat or lauding the Gentiles who would bring peace to Crete. It was not the heat, it was the anonymity.

"*Brutta gente*," is what an Italian would sadly murmur in the circumstances, addressing nobody in particular. "Horrible people." The antonym of this, in his frame of reference, would be *vip*, which no more means VIP than *night* means a place like Pacha. The Italian may think it means Milanese industrialists and Roman television personalities, but what it really, honestly means is people just like himself, *gente perbene*, ordinary, well-dressed people with good jobs, big mortgages, and aged parents. Like the bar of the Hotel de la Poste in Cortina in winter, Raya on Panarea is indeed full of them. Being nice children, they are a pleasure to watch as they drink, dine, and dance on the endless terrace overhanging a moonlit sea.

Unlike their autistic, rowdy, collectivist counterparts, they don't want to forget their failed lives and dissolve in the mass anonymity of the global march to progress. Indeed, what is there to forget if you are a twenty-year-old boy from Treviso? You have a loving family, a mother who phones you on the mobile to check if you've made it to the discotheque, and a beautiful younger sister who is already there, dancing with your best friend. All your friends are just like yourself, sowing their wild oats, and your wise father approves but reminds you that moderation is everything. If you want to become a painter or a playwright, instead of going into the family's lumber business, that's fine too, and even in faraway Notting Hill you know that you'll be supported and coddled as long as necessary. And let us not forget your grandmother, who is always there for you with her *pasta al forno*.

Indeed, what march to progress can there be when, twenty years later, you are a *vip*, dining at Raya on Panarea of a summer's night, and your sister is married to your best friend, and your mother still phones you four times a day, and you've long diversified your family business and now own the company that manufactures newsprint for *Corriere della Sera*? Of course their society reporters know you, and their photographers take pictures of you for the gossip column, and everyone in Milan says, "You know, I saw him at Raya. *Un night bellissimo.* Yes, it was *pieno di vip.*" And then the ignorant foreigners from *Paris Match* and *Harper's & Queen* hear all this, and repeat like parrots: "VIP! VIP! Just like Ibiza! But the food is Italian! *Bellissimo!*"

Ask me if I'm dreaming. Ask me if this is an old episode of *Father Knows Best*, or a chapter of *Doctor Zhivago*, or some other, still more fanciful, idealization of the good life in the eye of the proletarian hurricane. No, I tell you. This really is the truth. This really is how nice children play. This is the last cigar in Moscow. This is Italy.

XLII Venice

Hot, Cold and Tepid

The only substantive change to my character that I have observed over time is in the workings of the spleen, the abdominal organ once regarded as the seat of what is now called the negative emotions. When I was young, the objects of my hate were precious few, though of course I used to fulminate against them at the top of my voice; nowadays I seem to loathe just about everybody and everything, while saying little or nothing about it. This must be why one tends to imagine death as a kind of engulfing stillness, because by the time it comes, one has grown to despise the world so perfectly and completely that silent rage is the only commentary really suited to the occasion. Sometimes I think that if everybody's spleens functioned as well as mine, running like trains under Mussolini, we would all be living and dying in a more enlightened, Christian way.

Overheard in Piazza S. Marco the other evening, as the band in the middle distance, probably Florian's, let flow the tears for the vanquished in "The Hills of Manchuria." A microwave-quick female voice from a group of married couples, walking back to their hotel in Riva degli Schiavoni after a day of sightseeing: "Moe, Curly, and wass dee udder'n?" The creakier voice of a somewhat older woman, waddling excitedly beside the life of the party: "Leh-ah-rrry!" The life of the party, flirtatiously, to the three men dragging their feet behind them: "Larry, Curly, and Moe!" Provocative laughter from the three women. A man's voice in stern rebuke: "Now *don't* start, Maryann."

An issue of *Time* magazine opened at random, while in a doctor's waiting room, to an article headlined PUTIN'S BOLD MOVE: "Joining the West in its war on terrorism was the easy part. Now can he keep the generals happy and safeguard his country's backyard?" *By Maryann Bird. Could this be the same woman I overheard in Piazza S. Marco?* She quotes a Russian source: "'It's not NATO that now expands to the east,' writes Leonid Radzikhovski, a columnist for the weekly magazine *Itogi*. 'It's Russia that is drastically expanding to the west.'" To anybody with eyes the point made in *Itogi* would seem as plain as Larry, Curly, and Moe, but here's how Maryann extrapolates it:

> Directly or indirectly, Russia and the West may begin to sort out a broad range of issues: the expansion of NATO, the proposed U.S. national missile defense system, the Anti-Ballistic Missile Treaty, nuclear weapons capabilities, Russia's bid for membership in the World Trade Organization, debt repayments to Paris Club creditors and greater Western understanding regarding Russian tactics in Chechnya.

Maryann I and Maryann II, two peas in a pod, two housewives on a rampage, two faces of one and the same, uniquely Western creature. Truth to tell, if I felt totally free to vent my gloriously healthy spleen just now, I would be asking unanswerable questions like *Who allowed people like that into S. Marco?* or *Who will answer for the decision to fill reputable journals with housewifely twaddle?* With a twinge of something like remorse, I realize that such questions are not merely splenetic or rude, they sound elitist and even authoritarian. Alas, culture – in particular, the culture that democratic governments, their intelligence services, and their defence establishments lack so laughably – is more in tune with the workings of my spleen and other abdominal organs than with the editorial selection process at *Time* magazine or the CIA's recruitment procedures. The proof of this assertion is that World War III – the tepid war which in all likelihood will be won by Russia without a single shot being fired by a Russian hand – has in effect already been lost, before it ever began, by cheeky, flirty, and fat Maryann I, by important, Ivy-League-educated, and voluble Maryann II, and by a myriad other Maryanns whose different virtues and vices are less specific than the one characteristic they have in common, namely, their uniquely Western philistinism.

It is a quality easy to decry, but difficult to describe, although the first thing that springs to mind is the voice. It is always there, the Scourge of Air, as Catherine the Great of Russia called the tongue, raised above the music in the piazza and poised to slash the evening mist to ribbons. It is always there, the penchant for expressing what magazine editors call opinion, rooted as it may be in twentieth-century America's inability to discriminate between diversity and obesity, conservatism and conformity, originality and hooliganism, idleness and uselessness, intelligence and education, art and spectacle, knowledge and hearsay. It is always there no matter where you go, because housewifeliness, though originally a branded product of American prosperity, is now the globally audible soul of a more and more meaningless West.

Once, many years ago, in a restaurant called the Gay Hussar in London, I was given the famous Hungarian cold cherry soup. Ever since then, whenever some Mittel-European subject is broached, deep within myself I detect the impulse, which of course I have the sense to suppress immediately, to work the cold cherry soup into the conversation. And the reason I have not once mentioned that very odd dish, in all those years of convivial Mittel-Europa banter since I tasted it, is the stage whisper from my cultural conscience to the effect that I know nothing about it. That is to say, I don't know how it's made, when it's eaten, who eats and who doesn't eat it in its native land, and indeed whether there's such a thing as *hot* cherry soup.

The housewives who are losing World War III for civilization have no comparable restraining mechanism in place. They have no cultural conscience, and this characteristically twentieth-century American defect – which, consistent to the last, I would compare with the fatal atrophying of a vital bodily organ such as the spleen – permits them to be as free and easy, as stupid and trivial, as audacious and mendacious as the newspapers they read or write in, as the political leaders they work for or want to impeach, as the teachers in their children's schools and as the children themselves. From anthrax to Andropov, from computers to nuclear weapons, from peace treaties to Louis XIV, from the Venice Biennale to hot and cold cherry soup, they have an opinion about everything. If you disagree, just take a look at the *New York Times* one Sunday.

Throughout this tepid war, as I monitor the vital signs of Western political and cultural opinion – television commentators, government spokesmen, newspaper pundits, university experts – I am reminded of a wealthy Frenchwoman of my acquaintance who has married an artist because he *looks* artistic. I am reminded of the American book reviewer, who does not know what a poem is but always seems to know what the poem is *like*, and hardly bothers to conceal her childlike delight at the prospect of using her thousand words to tell the readers how to read it. I am reminded of the English waitress who has certainly never seen a cappuccino in her life but will place the scalding cup of brown cinnamon-scented dishwater in front of you with the aplomb of Phileas Fogg. And, saddest of all because this is where I now live, I am reminded of the Italian resort hotel manager, demonstrating her newly installed swimming pool the size of a Palm Beach bathing cap with yellow daisies and insisting that I agree with her it's American.

If the remarkable fact that it is women's voices that I hear in my head when I think of the housewives who now govern the West – anatomically male, many of them – should appear shockingly misogynist, do not blame any of my bodily organs. It is just that in times of crisis, such as war, pestilence, or famine, every society stands or falls by the way it chooses to deal with its share of babbling Maryanns, be they its Kerenskys, its Chamberlains, its McNamaras or Kissingers. Male, female, or neuter, these are the philistines of T. S. Eliot's prophesy, whose world of kitchen certitudes can only ever end with a whimper of submission. And, after what seems like centuries in the evolution of my spleen, it is indeed a surprise that I still have the requisite bile to jeer their indecorous life and inglorious fate.

... to deal with its babbling Maryanns

XLIII Venice

Masked Ambition

It is now Carnival. If you look at Venetian painting, where it is a recurrent theme, very occasionally among the profusion of masks and costumes worn by the revellers you will spot the fool's cap, the jester's conical hat decorated with bells or pom-poms. Nowadays the hat, sold on every street corner in a variety of colours and shapes throughout the winter, is without doubt the most conspicuous ornament of the day tourist, rather like the baseball cap in summertime. For foolishness is now *comme il faut* even among the working classes, and the louts descending on Venice in their hundreds of thousands are nothing if not conformist. On another social level, the court jester of today masquerades in Armani and pays full menu price for his plate of reheated tortellini at Cipriani with an American Express card.

At the Teatro Goldoni the other night, it has occurred to me that the old classical *commedia dell' arte*, which the Venetian playwright Carlo Goldoni appropriated, refined, and eventually supplanted, is no more a caricature of life than Monty Python. This makes me wonder whether one need not to have lived in Labourist Britain to appreciate that the Dead Parrot and the Ministry of Silly Walks are less lighthearted comic routines than vivid fragments of a comprehensive social puzzle which, were it ever fully assembled, would not look out of place in the work of a modern Dickens or Tolstoy. The pet shop sales assistant who does not want to sell parrots, and dreams instead of roaming the woods as a lumberjack, is not so much a whimsical figure of fun as the living and breathing lout of the very sort which now predominates among the not so young in the more prosperous nations of the world. As for the ministry in question – from whose exalted eminence men with names like Wim Kok can now teach three hundred million sales assistants *manqué* to dream strange dreams of liberty, leisure, and golden apples "where below another sky, parrot islands anchored lie" – it has, of course, opened for business in Brussels.

Nothing better illustrates the intense realism of old Italian character comedy – at least in its deservedly famous Venetian refraction – than the absurd harlequinade, which finally concluded in December to thunderous applause from an appreciative audience on both sides of the Grand Canal, that was my search for a new apartment to move to from Palazzo Mocenigo. Last summer, after a whole year of hopeful intrigue and angry entreaty, I finally crowed victory upon persuading the elderly, deaf, and vague owner of a suitably picturesque palazzo in S. Stae, across the Canal from the Casinò di Venezia, to sign the magical "*quattro più quattro*," the rent-stabilized residential lease that permits the tenant to occupy the premises effectively until his demise. Italian tenancy laws being what they are, only an elderly, deaf, and vague landlord would sign away his ancestral home to a total stranger almost certain to outlive him, and hence the only kind of legal arrangement on offer to foreigners here is the dud, one-year, market-pegged, tourist-accommodation lease that I, and the equally unfortunate Lord Byron before me, had at the Mocenigo.

I crowed prematurely, because when we signed in June, the S. Stae apartment was still occupied by the newly elected Mayor of Venice and his recently acquired wife. As far as I was concerned, this humourless and somewhat lumpy provincial politico was just a sitting tenant and a nuisance. Actually he was there to help his ambitious new wife to instruct the inhabitants of the city in highly important civic tasks, such as how to hold pigeons at bay without excessive cruelty to their persons, how to round off currency conversions from the laughably kaput Italian lira to the impeccably modern euro, and how to become better bootlickers, I mean citizens, of the European Community generally. And while it may well be that Signor Costa had been elected to his high post for a variety of tolerably valid reasons, on the basis of my personal experience I would be disinclined to believe that Signora Costa's youthful charm, natural simplicity, and disinterested kindness had been among them.

The first strategic decision jointly taken by Venice's first couple was to terminate their lease at Palazzo Duodo. A fourteenth-century Gothic palazzo, "no mod cons" – near the spot where Goldoni was born and round the corner from the churches of S. Giacomo dell' Orio, with Veronese's *Faith, Hope, and Charity* over the sacristy door, and S. Cassiano, with Tintoretto's *Descent into Hell* in the chancel – is most emphatically *not* a good address for the Modern Man who is an Important Figure with a Possible Future in European Politics, to say nothing of the Man with a Roman Wife Who Is Hell on Wheels. In Venetian *commedia dell' arte*, the self-important and loquacious *petit bourgeois* Pantalone hails from the Giudecca. It made perfect sense, therefore, that Venice's newest grandee and his missus were to move from S. Stae to a new, exclusive, and conspicuously modern condominium on the island, which was to be completed some time in the summer.

But come summer, strangely enough for the Modern Man with an Important Wife, who had tirelessly campaigned on the promise of rebuilding La Fenice on time and under budget, Pantalone's condominium was no more ready for occupancy than the charred remains of Italy's favourite theatre: not in July, not in August, not in September. Whereupon Mrs. Pantalone, though less touched by my homeless family's plight than by the plight of homeless families elsewhere, in Afghanistan for instance, took decisive action to avoid the political scandal that would almost certainly have unfolded if our elderly, deaf, and vague landlord had taken the case to the local newspaper. She handed me the keys to a three-room office her husband was keeping in the same palazzo, with a benediction to the effect that I was welcome to whatever shelter this offered.

Reminiscent of the *commedia dell' arte* skit "La Casa Stregata," or "The Jinxed House," the production of the ensuing comedy calls for a split-level stage. Pantalone is told by the Doctor that he is ill and must take a house in the country for a change of air. The miserly Pantalone remembers at once that he owns a place in Castello – in Monopoly terms, this is like remembering that you own a tenement in the Bronx – which is rented to Arlecchino. He throws out the hapless ingénu and, looking forward to his *petit bourgeois* lungs devouring all that free Castello air, moves in himself. Whereupon Arlecchino's friends come together to persuade Pantalone that the house is haunted, and night after night he is forced to pay the princely sum of four *zecchini* to the psychologically astute Brighella playing the scary ghost.

On the upper level, Pantalone contemplates the fate of Venice's pigeons and the future of the euro while Mrs. Pantalone stirs away at the cocktail of his political ambition, one part Mother Teresa to six parts Lady Macbeth. On the lower level, Arlecchino and friends plot ghostly revenge on the infernal couple. Pulcinella, the owner of the palazzo, and all the comic *zanni* run back and forth between the two levels, scrambling on top of one another like the famous Brustolon angels on the vase supports in the grand ballroom of Ca' Rezzonico, tripping over the furniture and falling over in unimaginably funny ways. After more than three months of such slapstick, a veritable fool's cap on more than a year of agonized pantomime that preceded it, imagine my relief when, one dark day in late November, *deus* finally came out of the *macchina da caffè* to intervene on the side of the downtrodden. Over an espresso in Campo S. Luca, a friend of mine, young Hugues L—, told me of a family house of theirs, Palazzo Contarini-Michiel, that was in the process of being vacated by the Greek Consul in Venice after some twenty years of neglectful occupation. And yes, his father would let me have the same "*quattro più quattro*" that the Consul had.

The fifteenth-century palazzo stands on the Grand Canal next to Ca' Rezzonico, the very grand house where Robert Browning lived and died, and it is under its roof, needless to say – because this is Italy, where every good *commedia dell' arte* plot must always have the happy ending conducive to healthy digestion – that I am now writing this proclamation of final and quite irreversible triumph. When I told Lady Pantalone that I had made other arrangements, and was no longer in need of her ambiguous hospitality, the copperplate Roman look on the blank of her ivory-laid face was recompense enough for the eternity I had spent in addressless anguish. Curtain, applause, *polenta* for the actors.

… contemplates the fate of Venice's pigeons and the future of the euro

XLIV Milan

The Book of Italian Excuses

A decade ago, Celeste Dell'Anna, to this day the only interior designer in Milan with a world reputation and a beautiful wife, was doing our new house in Knightsbridge. We became great friends, initially because I appreciated the tragic spectacle of this man of culture being baited, like some great white stag personifying the Italian rococo, by a pack of London builders who seemed to have been disgorged by Tolkien's subterranean regions. Some were dwarves, others impossibly gaunt; some had warts, others long hair the colour of pigsty straw; some spoke not at all, others were full of palaver; but the one thing all these barbarians had in common was the kind of sylvan, northern, autistic stupidity that is now the chief distinguishing characteristic of the socially displaced and the ethically disenfranchised.

A pupil of the legendary maximalist Renzo Mongiardino, Celeste went on to design yacht, aeroplane, and helicopter interiors for the Agustas, for the Aga Khan, and for the King of Spain. But this was his first job in England. Long used to reconciling the conflicting demands of space, personality, and skill, he valiantly tried to suppress the dawning realization that he was no longer in St. Moritz, that none of his fancy footwork now mattered, and that this time round, in the suitably rustic idiom of the Russian proverb, the scythe had hit a stone. The technical sketches he executed in brown chalk on the stripped yet evermore grimy walls of Victorian hallways and cloakrooms looked more plausible than Renaissance inventions, and each possessed the charm of a museum Watteau; but the ulotrichous workmen either ignored them, to make time for their off-track bets and their electric tea kettles, or plastered them over with copies of the *Sun*, their window on the enchanted Thule of bestially guiltless leisure where the woman's breast was always a size larger than the footballer's head.

In the evenings I drank with Celeste, who had come to accept that alcohol was less unaesthetic than anaesthetic, and while at times a symptom of barbarism, always an antidote to some of its more unsettling effects. When thus tranquillized, Celeste would invariably try to persuade me to write a book about the experiences we were living, advice I could have done worse than followed. He insisted that I should entitle it *The End of the Day*, as this was the phrase, beloved of every stratum of the proletariat in Britain, that he had come to loathe and fear most. To him, *Workers of all nations, unite!* or *Avanti, popolo, alla riscossa!* were history's dusty abstractions, but whenever he heard an unwashed plumber tell him that "A' th' end o' the die, Mr. Delfini, it won' mike much o' a diff'rins if the wa'ah mine *does* run down, 'cos iss *beige*, innit, same's the wall gonna buy," he would tremble in incomprehension and terror like a French nobleman in view of the scaffold. And when, at the end of the day, his own workmen from Bergamo finally arrived to finish the decoration, and I saw their thoughtful faces, their identical, crisply pressed blue overalls, and their tools neatly arranged in mahogany cases, I too felt ennobled and ever so slightly guillotined. They worked like

... the memory of Celeste's art chastens the incorrigible mocker

Sisyphus, chivalrously insensible of the truth that imposing their precious superstructure on the rude base left behind by the troglodytes of the north was as inutile as raising a marble bust on a plinth of cardboard.

Years have passed. I have become godfather to Celeste's son. London is now only a gambler's memory, selective, capricious, and blind to the ruinous distinction between last week's big loss and last year's big win. The other night we drank together again, this time at his studio in Milan, and as I regaled him with my stories of apartment hunting in Venice and house restoration in Palermo, he again chided me for not having written about our London experiences. He wanted to know what sort of book I might be thinking of these days, now that I had come to live in his country. I joked that the best-seller the world really craves at the moment is *How to Live Well on $1 Million a Year*, for the simple reason that those with the means to make themselves manifestly unhappy are so bad at mastering them. But then it occurred to me that there was, in fact, a variant of *The End of the Day* that was relevant to my present condition.

This would be called *The Book of Italian Excuses and Lies*. Neither Celeste nor I ever supposed that *The End of the Day* would become some sort of diatribe against the national character of the inhabitants of Britain, and we accepted that no treatise on hygiene, no diachronic study of climate, and no history of education could ever explain the shocking fact that British workmen wear no underwear. Similarly, in this book I would not tackle the larger generalities – such as the really shocking fact that just about every Italian, of whatever age, believes that his country has fought on the winning side in World War II – concentrating instead on the quotidian of small evasions and white lies, the fibbing, mercurial, hypochondriacal continuum of men's private lives in which the Italian character comes to the fore.

A few days ago I went into a shop to ask if they had any pickled gherkins, and I want to give the owner's reply verbatim. "Pickled gherkins *as such* I do not have at the moment," he said with the dignified deliberation that one always finds so becoming in a shopkeeper, "but I do have pickled capers, which is a kind of gherkin only a little smaller and rounder." My laughter offended him: "You will not find the *other kind* in any shop, sir," he said haughtily, "but if you insist I can always ask the wholesaler if we can have that" – I was sure he had something rude like "*porcheria*" on the tip of his tongue – "specially ordered for you." For the morality of much Italian lying is predicated on the ready offence to be taken at the slightest suggestion that one is not telling the truth, an attitude that, at least to the Russian Orthodox eye of my housekeeper, makes even ordinary law-abiding Italians akin to horse-thieving Gypsies.

The attitude goes well with the ubiquitous persona that may be called the *cavaliere servente* – it is not for nothing, after all, that Italy is famous for her lovers – who first woos and swoons, then yawns and switches off his portable. Ubiquitous, I say, because the spirit of the distracted lover holds sway over the behaviour of the architect and the lawyer, the hospitable host and the polite guest, the promising politician and the enthusiastic voter. In the morning the man of the moment is full of exquisite dreams, and it seems he can think of nothing besides his new mistress, his new vocation, or his new plan; come afternoon, neither inviting this nor aware that it contravenes his earlier state of mind, he suddenly feels himself drawn to some other object of interest glistening in the middle distance, be it a splendid racecar in a magazine advertisement or a jewelled collar round the neck of a passing poodle; come evening he feels weary of it all, and besides he has a chest cold coming on, or else the clams had disagreed with him; *lascia perdere*, he mutters ruefully, to hell with all those women, plans, and dogs, I am going to call my mother and then have myself a nice cup of camomile tea.

Hence the malingering for which the nation is famous. Walk into any Italian pharmacy and you will find yourself in the town's most fashionable salon, where everyone is a grandee though some are grander than the rest, and where the social competition turns on the issue of just whose diseases are more evanescent. The butcher's daughter feels that she has a sore on her cheek that could lead to complications, and the beauty of it is that the sore is *invisible*; five minutes of discussion. Not to be bested by a mere butcher's daughter, the chartered accountant's brother complains of a *constriction* in his lungs, one that, moreover, he experiences only at carnival time; five minutes of animated discussion, followed by the purchase of vitamin capsules. Then an unknown lady in a voluminous fur coat, holding her own against all comers, announces that she simply has not been *well*; ten minutes of highly animated discussion, with the pharmacist coming out from behind the counter to make more elbow space for philosophical expostulation. By lunchtime closing, everyone who matters in society – that is to say, everyone who is truly delicate – has been gravely ill and miraculously cured.

This, after all, is the aboriginal Catholic country, where the wind blows where it list. Here, cause and effect are not linked with that scientific rigour, or that banal literalism, which has made northern Europe what it is at the end of the day, namely, honest yet ugly, straight yet plain, educated yet stupid, rational yet credulous, efficient yet shoddy, heated yet cold, consistent yet discontented. And the funny thing is that of course you *can* be in two places at the same time, if you are an Italian lover, saint, or plumber; and if, like the sweet little *bambino* you were born, you are the apple of your mother's eye, you can easily be at once sick and well; while to any lawyer your case is both A and not-A, and *lasciamo perdere* the excluded middle; and besides, who is to say that you cannot be a talented painter one day and decide to grow *radicchio di Treviso* the next?

For the freedom to sin, which presupposes the telling of lies, and to repent, which condones the invention of excuses, is the supernatural, perennial, adamantine fabric that lines the motley and threadbare robe which is the Italian character. I am quite sure that the book I could write on the subject, *The Book of Italian Excuses and Lies*, would make that character even more of a laughing stock than it already is the world over. But the memory of Celeste's art and his workmen from Bergamo chastens the incorrigible mocker, the faint outline of the Cathedral on the far side of the cynic's wineglass makes him lose heart, and the trusting approach of barefooted Mediterranean spring makes the satyr's harp fall soundless to the ground.

XLV Palermo

North and South

The proprietor of the restaurant M— A—, known as Ricotta, likes to share with his intimate friends – for the most part fecund, avuncular family men who, between them, did upwards of a thousand years in the high-security Section 2 of the city's thistle-shaped Ucciardone jail, awaiting trial on accusations of various victimless crimes, usually involving government building contracts, accusations that, *mirabile dictu*, invariably came to nothing – the story of his first and last visit to Venice. As I know nothing of the Sicilian dialect which he speaks – except how to inject the right note of lazy indignation in the retort *"Ma qual' Mercan'?"* whenever the taxi driver ventures, "American?" – the story is simultaneously translated into the soulless standard Italian of the mainland by several voices in the womanless crowd.

My friend Maglio O— explains that the Sicilian spoken by our hero is high Palermitan, which is far more different from the dialects of the countryside than, say, the sounds of Tuscany are from those of Umbria. Thus, where Ricotta refers to himself as *io*, his social counterpart in Madonie, some sixty kilometres away, would say *ia*; in Salemi, 70 km. from the city centre, he would say *ieu*; in Marsala, which is 30 km. from Salemi in the same province of Trapani, he would say *eu*. In the province of Caltanissetta, 110 km. away, he would say *iè*. In Catania, in the eastern part of the country 200 km. away from Palermo, he would say *iù*.

"I guess you could say they saw me coming," Ricotta warms up to his subject, always with the same self-effacing *rallentando*. "I tell you what happened. I'd just got off at Piazzale Roma, and there's this newspaper stand right in front. So I start picking out postcards for my little ones, two hundred lire each, it said, views of Venice. I get six, one was for my wife, and what does that make? A thousand two, of course. Now, I give the fellow a thousand five, and I say to him, 'You all right with that, boy?' And straight away he hears my voice he bolts from his hole, to check how many I'd taken. Which is six."

Here Ricotta pauses to catch his breath, and in the silence of the crowd one hears his asthmatic lungs creaking like some terribly clever hydraulic apparatus that the ancient Romans left behind. "Then I say to him, if you're going to be like this about it, give me back my change. So the fellow turns to go back to his hole, but I'm already pretty bothered, so I pull out my knife" – Ricotta pulls out a folding knife the size of a small banana – "and I tell him, you'd better count well, you bucket of garbage, because I want my change to the last lira! So he gives me the three hundred back, and then I go *woosh*! And just toss it into the canal. It's what I did, I swear on my mother's grave that's just what I did. God knows I must've been angry by then, to have seen myself treated like some kind of criminal just because I talk as we do. And by that *garbage*!"

It is not so much the dramatic sacrifice of 15 cents in American money for the honour of his people as the evident fact that this, indeed, is the old voyager's only halfway vivid recollection of

...here's the old buck, the maverick warrior

magical Venice, that elicits hoots of approbation and slaps on the shoulder from Ricotta's listeners, who fall over one another to raise upturned fingers over the back of his balding head: "*Cuinnutu!*" Yes, here's the old buck, the maverick warrior with more horns on him than a man can count, the ageless symbiosis of Minotaur and his slayer, the virile *cornuto* with masculinity all tangled up in disingenuousness, the mythic simpleton who's been to Hades and wound the infernal lot of them round his gnarled left pinkie. He may talk an even funnier Italian than the rest of them do, but *he* has never seen the inside of the Ucciardone thistle. And as for the money, no need to worry about the owner of the best fish joint in *Sette Cannoli*, or Seven Spigots, as this part of town is called, because every jeweller in downtown Palermo knows old Ricotta's got pillowcases of the stuff stashed away, and not in lire, either.

What's in it for me, you may wonder. The Palermitan answer is, protection. For the fact is that, even after all these years spent in Italy, I'm still of a divided mind on the question of which picturesquely neglected corner of it will last the longest – and will protect me best – in the coming total eclipse of European civilization. First I thought it could only be Rome, which had already fallen so many times that another tumble would hardly matter. Then it was Venice, which the world had decided was sinking and hence in all likelihood would keep well away from. Now a part of me feels that in these apocalyptic times I will need to shroud my fugitive soul in the rustic logic of proud old Ricotta and his *cornuto* companions, because Venice – Palermo's great antipode and coeval within the besieged microcosm of what is now left of the living Europe – yes, even Venice is now in peril.

The other day the Italian parliament approved the infamous Moses Project, which involves stealing billions in state funds under the Berlusconian pretext of constructing inflatable dikes to control the Adriatic tide, a scheme that is certain to subvert the unique ecology of the Venice lagoon. That same week, a new directive from Brussels specifically forbade the selling of *germoglio* artichokes cultivated on the island of Sant'Erasmo, beloved of the locals under the name *castraure*. Well, did a single Venetian pull out his bone-handled silver fruit knife and swear vengeance on the tomb of his beloved maternal great-aunt from Sovizzo, near Montecchio, in the province of Verona? Did a single stallholder at the Rialto market shout "Judas!" as he threw a fistful of euros in the face of a passing *politico*? No, the gentlemen of the north among whom I've been living are too refined for violence, which explains why the town is full of lawyers. Only a thick *terrone*, a country bumpkin from the southern boondocks jabbering in his dialect, and naturally *maleducato*, would make a scene, which explains why so many healthy young men prefer selling postcards with views of Venice to growing vegetables in the Veneto.

The reliance on dialect, all but absolute throughout Sicily, is both the yardstick and the backbone of the social organism to which I look for protection as an individual. And, speaking of the backbone, the cut of beef called *lombata* in standard Italian is *lombo* in Bologna, *roast-beef* in Milan, and *sotto filetto* in Turin; in Palermo it's *trinca*. The *fesa* is called by that name only in Verona and Turin, while in Bologna and Florence it becomes *scannello*, *schenello* in Genova, *rosa* in Milan; in Naples it's *natica* and in Palermo it's *sfasciatura*. The term *pancia* is only used by butchers in Verona, while in Florence they say *falda*, in Milan *biancostato* or *bamborino*, in Turin *spezzato*; in Naples, *pancettone* and in Palermo, *panza*. The part called *reale* is known as *polso* in Florence, *matama*

… or shall I stake my all on a life with sultry Sicilia

in Genova, and *fracosta* in Rome; in Naples it is called *locena* and in Palermo it is *spineddu*.

A recent survey conducted by the government census agency Istat, entitled "*I cittadini e il tempo libero*," has shown that 92.3 percent of all Italians are able to speak both the standard language and their local dialect. A mere 44.1 percent speak standard Italian at home, though 72 percent use it when speaking to strangers, "a vast improvement on the 1950s when only 33% did." Women are more reluctant than men to speak in dialect, either at home or in the presence of strangers. None the less a clear majority of the population, 52 percent, are capable of "fully expressing themselves" by means of "local language" alone.

Viewed topographically, the picture is pellucidly clear. Exclusive or predominant use of standard Italian is typical of the central provinces, with 63.2 percent, and those of the northwest, with 59.4 percent, while in the south three out of four inhabitants "eschew the language of Dante" whenever they can help it. Florence and Tuscany score the highest, 83 percent, while Venice and the Veneto region – encouraging for one who has just signed a long lease on a palazzo at Ca' Rezzonico – rain acerb disdain on all comers with the mainland low of 42.6 percent, lower even that the Alto Adige and Friuli. But then there's Ricotta, who can only count in Italian, up to a hundred thousand lire for freshly made linguine with rock lobster.

So, in the cynical idiom of the Duke of Mantua, this one or that one? Shall I stick it out, in the long term, with the sophisticated, cool, and headstrong Venezia, or shall I view her as a mere holiday escapade, a shipboard romance, an afternoon in a swing in the sprawling garden of a Palladian villa in the Brenta? For I confess to have a great fear of being cuckolded by her long ere we marry – why else did the Doges wed the sea every summer? – and it may be wisest to regard her with the same caution that her own fishermen reserve for her deceptively placid waves. Or shall I stake my all on a life with sultry Sicilia, hanging out in open-air cafes with her fathers, brothers, and sons, drinking coffee the colour of her gently rounded eyes and shouting "*Cuinnutu!*" whenever one of the men tells a wondrous tale of his exploits in some sunken Atlantis?

Perhaps I should try two-timing the both of them. Or would that be too – I don't quite know how to put it – too *Venetian*, somehow?

XLVI Venice

American Italics, or Revelation According to P.T. Barnum

> Ye are the salt of the earth: but if the salt
> have lost its savour, wherewith shall it be
> salted? It is thenceforth good for nothing,
> but to be cast out, and to be trodden under
> the foot of men.

As in some picaresque dream, the carousel that has been spinning out a tale of broken hearts and mistaken identities begins to slow down, the roulette wheel grows disenchanted with the last bourgeois revolution, and all of a sudden even the drum of the concrete mixer that is shadowing the Venetian's limousine all the way to the airport grinds to a gravelly stop. Lady and gentlemens, as my friend Gusov might say when in a pompous mood, I have been to Las Vegas, I have seen the beginning of the end, and I now know what the salt that has lost its savour tastes like. But meanwhile, like the dove with the olive leaf in its beak, I am returning to the ark of the narrative, and now the stillness and the smell of the sea are once more all about me, and already the water taxi is going full throttle under a waning moon that looks like a *piano nobile* badly divided among the brothers after a century and a half of family quarrels.

The place where we chose to stay could have been Augustan Rome *constructed in a majestic Greco-Roman style*, that is to say Caesars Palace, or Italy as Mazzini invented it and hence of no particular period, the Bellagio. *More than a thousand fountains, enhanced by music and lights. A state-of-the-art fog and audio systems. The Bellagio Gallery of Fine Art. Synchronized swimmers, divers, contortionists, trapeze artists, and others perform incredible feats. This facility is a non-commercial venue dedicated to the presentation of high-quality art exhibitions.* Or it could have been Paris – Paris, France – because there is one in Vegas, you know, complete with *the Eiffel Tower tour and Restaurant. Rustic finishes have been applied to ensure that each structure is unique and appears appropriately weathered for its age. The ambience is very European and charming, and the shops are provincial and unique.* Or I could have gone to the Excalibur. *Ever dream of traveling back in time to an age of jousting knights? This is your opportunity to enter the world of King Arthur.* Or else we could have stayed at the Tropicana, *a bit of Polynesia in the desert, with its colorful prints and wood-and-bamboo furnishings.*

But for reasons no longer obvious even to my longtime gambling companion, I had decided on the *upscale Venetian, along nearly a quarter-mile of Venice's famed Grand Canal, where for a small fee you can take a gondola ride and be serenaded in an authentic gondola by a singing gondolier wearing authentic gear.* We breakfasted at a restaurant called *Tintoretto*:

I suppose I ought to say something about the gambling. Not contented with having added an extra number to the wheel, thus boosting the house's advantage over the player from 2.7 to 5.26 percent in what they call "American" roulette, these P. T. Barnums have even redesigned the single-zero "French" roulette wheel – known throughout Europe, incidentally, as "American" – to make the wells more shallow, the frets flatter, and the centre cone lower. Hence what, in the better London clubs, is still a suicidally dangerous game of observation, extrapolation, and inference, is here reduced to a mechanized variant of lotto, ideal for old ladies who wish to lose their life savings slowly, one dollar at a time. In London, betting a thousand pounds a spin is barely respectable, while here, after Gusov and I had kept $1000 on the layout for an hour, a crowd something like a hundred strong gathered to gape and bleat.

The place I visited is not the old utopia of gangsters' craps-shooting molls, of wedding chapels and cash loans, of tail fins and bail bondsmen. It is the new America, a place where actuary tables and shopping malls are churches, museums, and concert halls, a state of mind where the lowest common denominator of the chemically tranquillized millipede defines all beauty, all culture, and all history. *127,000 hotel rooms, more than New York or Paris. The finest collection of owner-operated restaurants in the world. Premier gaming in a Venetian palazzo.* It has nothing to do with gambling – that is to say, with risk – and everything to do with the pursuit of idleness, which is the true revolutionary ideal of mankind. More than once during my sojourn I was reminded of the scene in Lampedusa's *The Leopard* when the Prince is approaching Palermo besieged by Garibaldist rabble, passing the shuttered convents and the domes of the darkened monasteries:

> And at that hour, at night, they were despots of the scene. It was against them really that the bonfires were lit on the hills, stoked by men who were themselves very like those living in the monasteries below, as fanatical, as self-absorbed, as avid for power or rather for the idleness which was, for them, the purpose of power.

… the famous landmarks that make Venice the most beloved

The idleness to the pursuit of which the city – and the rich and powerful state, richer than Babylon in the Revelation and armed with nuclear missiles, that emulates, inspires, and sustains it – are dedicated, is officially called *entertainment*. Here, even two-bit hookers may only advertise in the Yellow Pages as "entertainers," which, the taxi driver explained, is not really that confusing after all, since you are probably looking up "escorts" under *E* anyway. He had a *Taxi Rider's Bill of Rights* posted in his cab, I noted, which included "Air Conditioning on Demand." At the Venetian, *entertainment* was available on similar terms:

> Bringing high art and culture to Las Vegas, the Venetian is proud to be home to not one, but TWO prestigious Guggenheim museums. The 63,700 sq. ft. Guggenheim Las Vegas, designed by Pritzker-prize winning architect Rem Koolhaas, debuted in October 2001. Also open is the 7,660 sq. ft. Guggenheim Hermitage Museum which combines rare works of art from both the Guggenheim and the State Hermitage Museum from St. Petersburg, Russia. The initial exhibit features 45 masterpieces from the Impressionist and Early Modern eras, some never before seen in the United States. Visitors can also take in headlining acts at the state-of-the-art, four-level Venetian Showroom.

"If the CIA can merge with the KGB," Gusov murmured ruefully when I pointed to the press release, "I do not see why the Hermitage cannot merge with the Guggenheim."

Indeed, why not? And, once you're at it, why not *recreate with painstaking exactness*, against the picturesquely lunar backdrop of the atomic testing ground that is the Nevada Desert, *the famous landmarks that make Venice the most beloved, romantic city in the world?* Let us be serious, lady and gentlemens! Did not the wise men who built Yale University, for instance, so reason, aiming to *recreate with painstaking exactness* what they supposed was the ageless Gothic of Eurford and Eurbridge, and all the things that made them *the most beloved, romantic seats of higher learning on earth?* Did not the instigators of the American Revolution so reason, wishing to *recreate not one, but TWO great chapters of history, from the excitement and the high drama of Runnymede, with King John and the valiant band of barons that rise up against him in authentic period costume, to the great revolutionary upheaval of the English Civil War and the prestigious ambience of Sir Oliver Cromwell?* And did not the CIA so reason, when it decided to merge with the KGB in all but name *to recreate with painstaking exactness the democratic structures of a free country in totalitarian Russia, culminating in an award-winning, 63,700 sq. ft. political façade behind which any number of dirty deals could be done between us and them?*

Lady and gentlemens, I will go further than my gambling friend Gusov. This is not the beginning of the end. This is the end.

... this is the end

COLOPHON

Original images by Gusov printed as silver gelatin bromides
Designed by Sally McIntosh, typeset in Monotype Baskerville
Tritone separations by Christiaan Verraes
Printed at 300-line screen by St Ives Westerham Press
on 148gsm Monadnock Dulcet Smooth
Bound by Hunter & Foulis

Hurtwood Press Limited
Stoke House, Snatts Hill, Oxted, Surrey RH8 OBL
www.hurtwoodpress.com